Annie's Loo

the Govan origins of Scotland's
Community Based Housing Associations

Raymond Young

ARGYLL✤PUBLISHING

Argyll Publishing
Glendaruel
Argyll PA22 3AE

www.argyllpublishing.co.uk

in association with
Scottish Federation of Housing Associations

This publicaton has been made possible through
the support of the following:

- Cruden Group

- Hypostyle Architects

- Martin Aitken & Co, Chartered
  Accountants

- Reid Associates, Chartered Quantity
  Surveyors

- Scott Bennett Associates, Consulting Civil
  and Structural Engineers

- Anderson Bell Christie Architects

- Assist Architects

British Library Cataloguing-in-Publication Data.

**A catalogue record for this book is available from
the British Library.**

ISBN 978 1 908931 20 7

Printing
Bell & Bain Ltd, Glasgow

Dedication

This book is dedicated to the unsung heroes of the early days of what became the Glasgow Rehabilitation programme – the residents of Govan. In particular Annie Gibbons, Sheila O'Halloran, Effie McGeorge, Carrie McLean, Peter Lewis and the other members of the Fairfield Residents Association without whom none of this story would have happened. They were willing to risk their homes, their savings, their relationships with their neighbours, and their time for an idea brought from outside. The way in which Glasgow's tenements were rehabilitated would have taken a very different form – and might even not have happened – if they had not decided to take a leadership role. Students, government officials, local authority officials and design teams can walk away; the residents – as is always the case with urban regeneration – have to live with the consequences. They provided the real leadership and they are the ones who should get any credit for any achievements that were to follow.

Foreword

SURELY it is strange to write a book about someone's loo! And is it not even stranger to think that forty years ago the *lack* of internal toilet and washing facilities in some housing in Scotland was a problem?

Flushing toilets had been invented centuries earlier, and provision was industrialised in the mid-nineteenth century. Bathrooms in new middle class homes had become the norm by the late 1800s, and were standard in new social housing from 1919.

By the 1970s we had skyscrapers and nuclear power, we'd sent astronauts – and dogs – to the moon, we could fly thousands of people daily across oceans. By the early 1970s pink, avocado and turquoise suites were even available for those privileged to enjoy the delights of internal plumbing! Yet in Scotland thousands of families still lived in tenement houses without an internal bathroom and toilet. What does this tell us about the priority we attach to ensuring decent living conditions for our people?

As Raymond Young reveals engagingly through the story of this endeavour in Glasgow, the solution was partly technical, partly financial and partly social. The achievement of modest ambitions to solve a basic problem in one community in Govan demonstrated what could be done through a voluntary association led by the local community, encouraged and supported by enlightened govern-ments.

Their efforts created a model which was adopted and followed by other communities across Glasgow and more widely in Scotland, to create decent, warm, dry, affordable housing by rehabilitating older buildings and building new. Now, not only do all those houses have internal plumbing and flushing toilets, most are insulated to high standards, with efficient heating systems in place or being installed, and support services can be provided to those who need them. The associations and cooperatives of today are significant social enterprises, providing secure affordable homes for around half a million people in Scotland, more than one in ten households.

Who better to write about the origins of the Govan community-based housing association than the person who catalysed the project to bring indoor sanitation to the Glasgow tenement. Little did he know what was to follow!

Raymond Young emphasises serendipity and opportunity in bringing together the factors for success and he highlights the importance of leadership, at all levels. Arguably the combination of the two is what's critical. Opportunities come and go. It is leaders who use those opportunities and make things happen.

The author of this book is one such person and a key protagonist in the story of housing associations and cooperatives in Scotland, first in urban communities and later in rural Scotland. He has been lecturing about this for years with photos and stories – at conferences, to university students and to visitors from other countries. At last we've got him to write down the first part!

Dr Mary Taylor
Chief Executive
Scottish Federation of Housing Associations
January 2013

Contents

Govan Road
from the author's
flat/office at 964
Govan Road,
1971

Preface

'Life begins at 40 – but so do fallen arches, rheumatism, faulty eyesight and the tendency to tell a story to the same person, three or four times.'

Helen Rowland, American writer

FEBRUARY 10, 1972. 2.30pm. A big black car sweeps into Luath Street in Govan and stops outside number 10. Pat Lally, the chairman of Glasgow Corporation's Housing Sub-committee on Clearance and Rehabilitation (later to become a well remembered Lord Provost) steps out of the car, and walks up the three flights of tenement stairs to the house of John and Annie Gibbons. As he walks in the door he is handed the largest meringue he has seen, a cup of tea, and is invited to do a 'Clochmerle' by opening the bathroom that has just been installed. He declares the bathroom open in the presence of senior Government and Corporation officials, the press, TV and most importantly, a house full of excited local residents. His attempt to get back to his car is made difficult by the number of people climbing the stairs to see Govan's latest phenomenon – Annie's Loo.

For years this opening has been at the back of my mind for a book. It reads like a cross between a diary entry and the beginning of a novel. And it needs a little explanation before the rest of the story is told. . .

For a number of years people have been badgering me to write down the story of the early days of tenement rehabilitation and the impact that Annie Gibbons' bathroom, installed by the University of Strathclyde's ASSIST project, had on both the rehabilitation of Glasgow's tenements and on the type of housing associations in Scotland. Why badger me?

So let me get the personal story out of the way first, since it is a relatively personal book, although I hope that the audience for which it is written – housing association committee members and staff across Scotland, people interested in the development of housing policy in Scotland and those interested in events in Glasgow at a turning point in the fortunes of the city – will find it of interest.

It is over forty years since the central event of the story; most of the original participants have either retired or died. The origins of the Scottish community based housing associations tend to disappear into the mist (or is it myths?) of time. Before I forget my understanding of the story, it is worth writing it down. However, this is not a meticulously researched story, nor is it an objective analysis. It is a personal account by someone who was deeply involved in the events. I am not a fan of autobiographies; as one writer has commented, 'they are often a kind of personal spin doctoring'. However, this is a kind of an autobiography. So I apologise in advance if it misses out some people and events that others hold dear, or if it has a slant with which others disagree. Story telling always has a slant – and this one is no different. And I'll leave others to correct the mistakes!

I've spent most of my working life in social housing – starting with ASSIST, the tenement rehabilitation programme and the first of the community based housing associations that are at the heart of this story. I was fortunate in being the Director Scotland for the Housing Corporation during the time of the great expansion of the housing association sector in urban and rural Scotland, and then as Regional Director–North for Scottish Homes, being responsible for the development of a rural housing policy which saw major growth in local community associations in the more remote parts of Scotland. And I've kept an interest in the fortunes of housing associations through some years of teaching at Glasgow and Strathclyde Universities, as a board member (for a while Convener) of the Rural Housing Service, as a member of the Sustainable Development Commission and as the first chair of Architecture and Design Scotland. Even in my current role as an Advisory Board member of Historic Scotland, I remain in contact with the sector, following the impact that housing associations continue to make in maintaining our urban fabric (in this book I use the word 'urban' to cover settlements from 500 people upwards), in marrying new development and our historic places, and being leaders in the national drive for sustainability.

But I never planned it this way. My life seems to be characterised by a series of doors opening into places at the right time in which a slightly offbeat view was useful. For that is what I have offered. I was never a radical revolutionary; more of an evolutionary. But I hoped to make a difference.

Growing up in the 1950s and early 60s in Glasgow I could not but be aware of the housing conditions of large numbers of people in the city. My upbringing was in Maryhill in a relatively small middle class area; many of the people I knew (and some of my own relatives) lived in tenements with outside toilets. Delivering Christmas mail as a student in Maryhill took me up tenement closes with wooden floors to a landing, keeping out of the way of the rats. As the tramcar and then the bus rattled up and down Maryhill Road on my way to school, I learnt about a city where the housing conditions were quite different to my home.

I became an architect by chance. I had left school without enough highers to go to university. I worked as a wages clerk; one day my boss told me to 'stop doodling or go away and be an architect!' I did so – got into architecture school at Strathclyde University. In the midst of the course we had to do a 'year out'; which I did with a number of colleagues in Canada. That was the year that Martin Luther King and Bobby Kennedy were assassinated. I visited places like Newark, which had burned in anger in the riots that followed King's death, and a first nation reservation in Northern Ontario, and was affected by the intolerable conditions in which people were forced to live. I became less interested in designing opera houses (perhaps realising my own design limitations!), fell under the spell of Jane Jacobs (the author of *Death and Life of Great American Cities* – still one of my most important books) and started to ask questions about how people could have more control over their own environment. Back at the university at the tail end of the 1960s we found ourselves in a period of change, of challenges to what had become accepted practice – particularly in housing design and the role of the architect.

The issue that would not go away for me was summed up in my undergraduate thesis in 1969/70, which was called 'Design Participation' and included these statements (almost a manifesto):

> I believe that there is an important non-democratic aspect
> of our society, and that is the current right of the
> professional to make value judgements for the rest of
> society. I believe this pertains particularly to urban design. I
> feel that the future shape and design of the locality is best

left in the hands of the people who know it intimately; and that the role of the professional (architect, planner, etc) is that of a consultant, offering only professional advice.

Although it can be argued that there is at present a 'social conscience' in architecture (one only needs to look at the present preoccupation in architectural journals with public housing and its effects on users' lives) it is my contention that too much architecture is being built for other middle class educated, aesthetic-orientated architects to enjoy. There is a hope that the involvement of those who will use the environment will produce buildings with which the users will be more satisfied, even if the architectural quality does not measure up to the standards of the 'glossies'.

Over forty years later, although I would not perhaps use the same pompous youthful language, I would argue that much of what I said then remains true today. We still leave too much in the hands of the so-called 'professional' and many of the professionals still produce places where people are of secondary importance. That said, housing associations in Scotland have done much to demonstrate that given the chance and the support, local communities can provide the kind of physical environment that people want and enjoy. And many architects have changed their relationship with the community as client – many having worked with housing associations.

There is no mention of the words 'tenement' or 'housing associations' in the above extract from my 1969/70 thesis. There was no game plan. I had expected to do something different at the end of a short 6 month project with the New Govan Society. Even when the first bathroom (Annie's loo) was installed, there was little expectation of bigger things to come. There may have been wild ideas – like the first meeting with Ian Sloan, our quantity surveyor, when I gave him and his colleague Wallace Cuthbertson a vision of a series of architecture shops around the inner city. He left saying that I was mad. He remains a good friend!

There are also various strands to this story. They are largely woven together in Govan in Glasgow, and involve a series of players. The creation of community based housing associations brings together a university, the architectural profession, the church, the government, but above all what is now labelled the 'Big Society' – local community action. The Big Society was already in place in Govan long before the present Prime Minister was born – and the kind of community action that has been undertaken may not always conform to the image he wants.

How the book came about – and acknowledgements

I have been recounting the early days of tenement rehabilitation and housing associations for years and threatening to write a book about them. I even contemplated a proper academic study, with a lot of interviews and research. That came to nothing – partly because I always found something else to do, and partly because of my view of autobiographies.

In June 2006 Neil Baxter (now Secretary of the Royal Incorporation of Architects in Scotland – RIAS) asked me to tell the story for the 250th anniversary of the Govan Fair in the Pearce Institute. It was entitled '10 February 1972 – The Day Govan Started a Housing Revolution' and in preparation I began to dig through my own slides and the slide collection that I inherited from the Rev David Orr, who was minister of Govan Old Parish Church from 1960-1980. The collection of photographs that I have tracked down from those early days is perhaps another indication of the fact that there was not a grand plan; certainly not an intention to publish the story in future years. Even although David Orr took many slides (and I took some), we do not have photographs of many of the key events like public meetings or the opening of Annie's loo. The local paper, the *Govan Press*, regularly covered progress.

Since 2006 several opportunities have come along to develop the PowerPoint presentation; that required some research which has eventually led to this book. A major moment was when the Architectural Heritage Society of Scotland brought together Jim Johnson, David Whitham, Peter Robinson and me at a conference in 2009, and part of the story was subsequently published. My contribution was as ever a PowerPoint presentation. So in writing the book, the film came first!

A good deal of what is included in this book is either taken from papers written by me over the years or from other people who have written about the city and Govan. I am grateful to all who have contributed to the production of this book, wittingly or unwittingly – Jim Johnson, Peter Robinson, David Whitham, Theo

Crombie, David Martin, Phil McCafferty of ASSIST architects, the committee and staff at Govan Housing Association, Neil Baxter, Madhu Satsangi, Douglas Robertson and of course a large number of Govanites. I am particularly grateful to John Gilbert for the drawings, Mary Taylor, Chief Executive of the Scottish Federation of Housing Associations, who badgered and encouraged me more than most, and Diane Cooper of the SFHA who helped secure its publication. And of course, my wife Jean and the boys. If I have forgotten to mention your name – my apologies.

The format of the book

I have attempted to set the story of Annie's Loo in its context. Since it is about origins, we need to look first at the tenement, its role and the perception of the tenement in the history of Glasgow's housing. From a vantage point of 2012, it may be difficult to appreciate how revolutionary was the concept of tenement improvement.

Second, from the same vantage point in a time where 'star' architects dominate the profession and the public's understanding of the profession, I want to look at the important role played over the years by members of the architectural profession in changing our attitudes toward our cities – and in particular our appreciation of Glasgow's built heritage, and the moves from the 1960s towards greater public participation in the built environment.

The third important strand is Govan – a community within the city, but often feeling that it is not of the city. It has a proud and distinct history; by the time of our story it was in the early stages of a redevelopment programme, which was itself an important milestone in Glasgow's regeneration history. And central to this was a small but influential group from the community, instigated and led by church people, who were helping to shape the future of that shipbuilding community. They were then drawn into an architectural project with far reaching consequences, and they provided the first members of the first community based housing association – Central Govan Housing Association.

All of these come together to form the centrepiece – but not the end – of the story. That of Annie's loo itself. The timing of the event, the development of a full scale tenement improvement pilot thereafter and then the confluence of a number of political and institutional streams takes Annie's loo into a nationally supported programme that was to transform the city through the energies and commitment of local communities, and then to spread out across Scotland.

Today those energies and commitment are still present in the 150 RSLs (Registered Social Landlords to give them their twenty first century title) in all parts of the country which continue to provide good quality housing and a supportive environment for thousands of people, as well as a major contribution to the wellbeing of the different communities they serve. Localness is a distinctive feature of the Scottish RSLs.

Our story concludes by reflecting on what has happened to housing associations and some of the key players in the forty years since Annie's loo was opened.

I have written this as a story and have avoided footnotes and references to sources; the appendix sets out sources and further reading.

Rev David Orr

Glasgow is a tenement city – Victoria Road in the south side of Glasgow in the 1970s

Not all tenements were for the working class – these are 'posh' tenements in Hyndland

1. Glasgow and tenements

'An Englishman's home may be his castle but a Scotsman's hame is his close. Well, at least in Glasgow it was.'
                                                Jean Carlin, BBC Scotland archive

THE FIRST community based housing association (CBHA) was created in the tenements between Govan's historic churchyard and Fairfield shipyards. The tenement is clue to its origins, so some background on the tenement is where our story starts.

The Glasgow tenement is famous, sometimes infamous. The tenement defines the urban quality of the city, creating stone walled canyons in which lives are lived. It is the location for many negative images of the city – as told in stories such as *The Gorbals Story*, or in the TV detective series *Taggart*. However, the tenement was and remains the housing form in which generations of Glaswegians have been born, lived, played, loved and died.

At its finest the traditional tenement is basically a four storey building containing up to twelve flats, with an ashlar stone front and back in a building form that had been developed from the sixteenth century onwards; the design of which had matured to its peak in the late nineteenth/early twentieth century, and the building of which stopped abruptly in 1914 with the start of the First World War. Stone became too expensive and at the same time new patterns of housing were being considered. Tenements are still being built today – but we tend to call them 'walk up flats'! The continuing importance of tenements to the life of Scottish towns and cities can be seen in recent legislation designed to improve their management – the Tenements (Scotland) Act 2004.

No-one really knows where the tenement came from. It is a very different housing form from that in England and Wales where two storey terraced houses were the norm. Its origins may be Northern Europe, resulting from the days when Scotland was an independent state and part of a northern trading group of countries. It may go

Govan Housing Association collection

A shared 'outside cludgie' 1970

back further to the early days of Scotland when King David I brought town planners from the Low Countries to develop a series of Royal Burghs whose plans take the form of a living wall along a street that widens to create a market place. It may even be that the availability of stone as a building material encouraged vertical high density living. Whatever the origins of the tenement, it creates an urban fabric that gives Scottish towns and cities a distinctive and mainland European feel. And it is not simply a working class form of housing. In all Scottish cities there are large spacious and elegant flats that house middle and upper class families – some even have rooms for maids. Nor are all tenements of poor quality.

The heyday of tenement building in Scotland was in the fifty years before the First World War. In Glasgow, the city was growing at a phenomenal rate, as were the Burghs that surrounded it. Immigrants came from Ireland – flooding in as a result of the potato famine; immigrants came from the Highlands of Scotland – some the residue of the Highland Clearances; immigrants came from rural Lowland Scotland – forced to leave the land as a result of agricultural reforms. They all came to seek work in the growing industrial metropolis that was becoming the second city of the Empire. In the Burgh of Govan, in which much of our story takes place, and which did not become part of Glasgow until 1912, the population grew from 9,000 in 1864 to 90,000 in 1904 – an extraordinary growth rate paralleled today only by the industrialisation of countries like China.

These immigrants needed to be housed. This was long before social housing had been invented and the private sector had to rise to the challenge. The immigrants were poor, so low cost housing was built to rent and at a relatively low rent level. The housing was speculatively built, with investors seeking a financial return, and they left the day-to-day letting, management and maintenance to a property manager – the 'factor'.

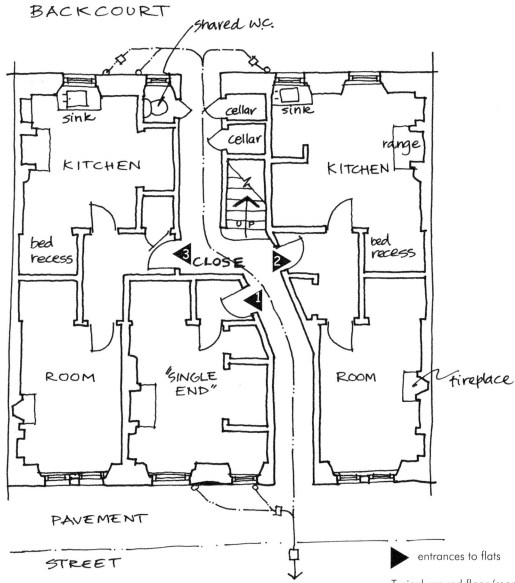

BACKCOURT

shared W.C.

sink

cellar

cellar

sink

range

KITCHEN

KITCHEN

bed recess

bed recess

3 CLOSE **2**

1

ROOM

"SINGLE END"

ROOM

fireplace

PAVEMENT

STREET

▶ entrances to flats

Typical ground floor 'room and kitchen' and 'single end' plan showing 3 flats with outside toilet, and (overleaf) upper floors in the same tenement – these are from the Govan study area

The flats were of one or two rooms ('single end' and 'room and kitchen' in Glasgow parlance), with shared toilets (first in the backcourt, then after around 1860 in toilet towers attached to the common stair with three flats sharing the one toilet ('outside cludgies'). The stair was accessed from the street by a passage (the close – which also became a commonly used term for the whole building – as in 'which close do you live up?') which linked the front of the building to the backcourt. Each flat was equipped with

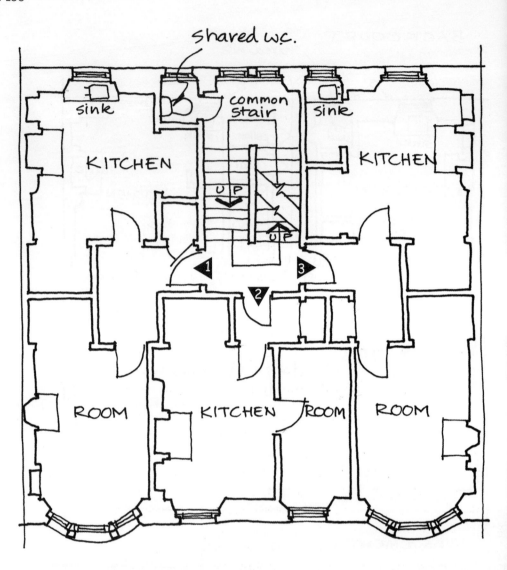

▶ entrances to flats

a kitchen sink (a 'jaw' box) with a cold water tap, a coal fire in the kitchen that doubled up as cooker (a kitchen range) including a small oven, and a shelf above with a rail to dry clothes. There would be a cupboard (a press) with shelves. In each room there was a recess measuring approximately 6ft x 4ft (1.8m x 1.2m) on which was built a platform which formed the base for a bed (the bed recess). In posher flats, the bed recess in the room could be inside a cupboard. Thus the immigrant rented a house that simply needed floor covering (the timber floorboards could be left bare), a few chairs, a table, crockery, pots and pans. When new, these flats may have been an improvement on the housing conditions that the immigrants had known, and superior to much of the older housing in the historic town centres.

On main streets, the ground floor would be occupied by shops, small businesses and public houses. The backcourts were separated on a close by close basis by a metal fence; each building had a washhouse for clothes washing (to be used weekly by each flat in rotation) and a bin store (the midden).

Within a typical tenemental area there would be some community facilities; some of them would be provided by the municipality. There would be the public washhouse, where it would be possible to bathe instead of using a 'tin bath' in front of the range and to do the weekly clothes wash if it was not done in the backcourt washhouse. The municipality (sometimes with funding from a private benefactor) would also provide places of self improvement like a library, or a park. Schools were built – mainly primary schools. The school leaving age was set at 14 from 1901 and only raised to 16 in 1973. Churches would provide for the soul; indeed some areas would operate a 'semi-religious' divide – Roman Catholics congregating near a chapel, Presbyterians and others elsewhere.

With small houses, life in a tenement involved living on the street. Children would play there – backcourts should only have been used when there was no washing hanging out to dry (an infrequent situation). People would congregate at the street corner – the men slipping 'occasionally' into the pub. The churches provided not only for the soul, but as a place for self improvement, for women to meet and learn, for Sunday School (many children were sent to Sunday School so that the parents could have some 'intimacy' time on a Sunday afternoon), for youth groups and places for older people. In a time when there were few alternatives, the churches provided both a religious and a social centre – for example, it was a Marist Brother, Brother Walfrid who established Celtic Football Club in 1887.

Since private transport was very expensive and public transport in its infancy, housing was provided close to employment opportunities. Thus, places like Govan had housing built right next to the ship yards, and the noise and pollution from coal fired heavy industries permeated the local community. These were not healthy communities. Smoke belching from furnaces and factories was only one hazard. Chemical effluents, horse manure (since most of the growing traffic was horse-driven), and poor sanitation combined with poor diet and low and expensive levels of health care led to low life expectancy – 44 for males and 46 for females in 1885.

So life in these high density housing areas must not be romanticised. These were harsh living conditions. It was bad enough to pile people on top of one another in small houses at high densities compared to the wider spaces of the rural life that many had left behind – in many cases unwillingly – to seek employment. But the employment offered was irregular, insecure, low paid and dangerous. Many heavy engineering employers cared little about health and safety, and the industries had appalling accident and death records. Workers could be hired and fired easily, and tribalism – religious, family, or geographical played its part – not just in getting a job, but in promotion prospects. Long hours were worked for low wages, and there was virtually no organised support for employees – trade unionism amongst semi-skilled and unskilled workers made little progress until the emergence of the New Unions in the late 1880s.

Is it any wonder that people took to drink to blot out the reality of life as much as to socialise? Violence – both domestic and inter-group – could be seen as another unacceptable response to the reality which ended the dreams of a new life in urban Scotland. The working class tenements of single ends and room and kitchens may have been built at the time when Glasgow was the second city of the empire, and was a city of great wealth. But the city displayed extremes of incomes – that great wealth was created on the backs of people who were paid some of the lowest wages in Britain. There was a great gulf between the rich and poor and a very small middle class. The plight of the urban poor was in complete contrast with the great financial rewards of the entrepreneurial elite who owned the industrial giants and who lived west of the industrial heartland in large villas on the edge of the city or further down the river in watering resorts.

For our story, that contrast in wealth and in housing conditions is to impact on the way Glasgow and the industrial towns around it develop, the impact on the provision of housing investment and ownership, on rent levels, and on the cultural attitudes towards tenements.

Russell Logan

Tenement back court

When they were built, the nineteenth century and early twentieth century tenements which characterise the city were an improvement on previous housing conditions. We need to go back a little in time to look at how these grew out of the mediaeval tenements in the core of the city.

Glasgow 19th century slums,
no. 80 High Street

2. First steps – architecture and housing join hands for social housing

'Every architect carries the utopian dream.'
Rem Koolhass, Architect

PUBLIC HEALTH was a major concern for nineteenth century reformers. The link between poor housing and poor health was well understood by the middle of the century – overcrowding, air quality and most importantly hygiene, water and sewerage. So housing became a social and political issue for reformers in the mid nineteenth century.

At that time poor people living in the historic core of the city of Glasgow were housed in some of the worst conditions in Britain. The rapid industrialisation had dramatically changed the '. . . cleanest and beautifullest and best built city in Britain' as Daniel Defoe described it in 1707. The demand caused by immigration created a shortage of decent and affordable accommodation, with tenement flats being subdivided and subdivided. Those that had been able to get out had fled to better places, leaving the most destitute to live in the dilapidated tenements which were severely overcrowded.

Overcrowding in Glasgow was higher than anywhere else in Britain. Attempts to control occupancy levels included the Town Council operating a system of 'ticketing' under powers given to it in the 1866 Glasgow Police Act. The 'ticket' on the door of the dwelling showed the number of people who could legally sleep there. One quarter of the city's families lived in one-roomed houses, often taking in lodgers as well to survive economically. These were rat-infested slums, with open sewers. One in five children born in them did not see their first birthday.

This was a time when 'the poor' became categorised into different levels of poor. Like a caste system, the Victorians developed the 'deserving poor' and the 'undeserving poor' – and as Carol Craig explains in her book *The Tears that made the Clyde*, in Glasgow this became a 'pecking order' of poverty, with the 'undeserving poor' themselves being regarded as the cause of the slums, rather than the victims. This attitude toward people on low incomes was to have a major (and maybe even continuing) impact on housing policy within the city.

Glasgow's first Medical Officer of Health was appointed in 1863, followed in 1866 by the City of Glasgow Improvement Act which established the City Improvement Trust. The Trust was controlled by the Glasgow Town Council (as it was until it became the Corporation of the City in 1895) and ultimately led to what we know as 'Council Housing'. This was also the start of what would now be regarded as a planned area regeneration programme – mainly demolition and new construction; not all of it new housing. The Trust was given powers to raise funds and to exercise the compulsory purchase of property. It set about clearing the worst slums, helped in no small part by the railways which were also acquiring the land in which worst slums were situated. There was of course no obligation on the railways to re-house – in many ways the railways exacerbated the problem by creating homelessness and even further overcrowding. At the heart of the mediaeval city was the University. This institution also took advantage of the railways looking for land, sold up and moved to Gilmorehill – and ensured that the students did not have to come in contact with the poorest of urban poor.

A tenement built by the City Improvement Trust in the early 1870s provided a model for later years – a mixture of two apartments and single ends, with shops on the ground floor and shared toilets on the half landing. By the late 1880s the Trust was building modern tenements in the heart of the mediaeval city, in places like High Street, replacing the older slums. Many, after further twentieth century modernisation, are still providing good homes and are now in the ownership of Glasgow Housing Association.

The Trust brought two issues together – sanitary reform and urban design. Sanitary reform was intended to improve the living conditions of the urban poor, to reduce both infant mortality and overcrowding, to provide decent water and sanitation (with the opening of the Loch Katrine Water Scheme in 1859 Glasgow had become a leader in the provision of free clean water). The opportunity for sanitary reform was seized upon by the City

City Improvement Trust
properties on High Street

Architect John Carrick and other members of the architectural
profession to design a modern city. Glasgow Town Council did not
regard itself as a 'provincial' city. It had ambitions and looked to
mainland Europe for models to follow (shades of earlier Scotland
and David I's European influences). In the nineteenth century, the
influence was to come from Paris as rebuilt by 'Baron' Haussmann.
Following a visit to the French capital by the City Fathers, a new
Glasgow was to grow from the ashes of the old one, with wide
streets in the grid iron pattern now typical of the city as a whole.
But it was at the cost – unlike Edinburgh – of removing virtually
the entire mediaeval city. It was not to be 'picturesque' – it was to
be modern!

Not everyone agreed. For example, in Govan where similar

Govan Housing Association collection

883 Govan Road – Brotchie's 'modern residential barrack'

developments were taking place – albeit on a less monumental scale and maintaining the mediaeval street pattern – T.C.F. Brotchie, writing his *History of Govan* in 1905, commented on the demolition of 'a quaint old cottage' and its replacement with a 'modern residential barrack'. That 'barrack' is now a Grade B listed building. And it is in the ownership of Govan Housing Association. *Plus ça change!*

The brave new world was to be reinforced by the Housing of the Working Classes Act in 1885 which provided that local authorities could borrow from the Exchequer monies for housing construction – no grants or subsidies. Inevitably the issue of affordability arose. In 1886 John Carrick was asked to design houses with a rental not exceeding one shilling and three pence per room per week. He pointed out that rents in Liverpool and Manchester (where there had been further study visits) were much higher, and the construction costs lower – mainly because they used brick, not stone. Rent levels were adjusted upwards; the relationship between income and rents does not appear to have been taken into account since the average working class income in Glasgow was lower than in Manchester and Liverpool. The current twenty first century debates about quality, affordability and procurement are but a continuing story down the years.

The City Improvement Trust was wound up in 1901, having completed some 1600 dwellings (although that housed just over one in three of those displaced by the clearances). But the Trust was a model for future social housing, both in terms of providing better affordable housing and of urban design. The role of the local authority as the main provider of social housing was the outcome of the Royal Commission on the Housing of the Industrial Population of Scotland, Rural and Urban, in 1917.

The Royal Commission had been set up in 1912 following a series of delegations from mining communities. Its work took place during a period of serious strife. The First World War brought matters to a head. There was an influx of workers to the munitions factories and so demand for housing grew. Inflation was already an issue; household costs were rising sharply. Housing scarcity was reflected in rapidly increasing rent levels, and these were seen by many (and in most cases correctly) as a blatant example of war-time profiteering. With the men away at the war front, and those who were not away working long hours to provide ships and munitions, it was the women who faced the challenge – and did so with the support of the new Independent Labour Party. The women organised themselves into tenants' committees for solidarity and began a series of rent strikes. Non-payment of rent became a national issue. When landlords tried to take the women to court to get them evicted, the landlords were lambasted as unpatriotic, and public support increased.

Govan was at the forefront of the rent strikes. One of Govan's great heroines – Mary Barbour – set up the first 'Govan Housing Association'. Its purpose was not to provide houses. The Association, like other 'Women's Housing Associations', was to provide support for the rent strikes. Eventually the Government was forced into passing the 1915 Rent Act to control the level of rents (although it may be that the Government felt forced into the situation because it feared a Bolshevik style uprising and simply tried to buy time).

The Royal Commission was to have the major impact on how our housing was to develop during the post Great War years. Having reviewed in depth the housing conditions across Scotland, it argued that to a great extent the industrial unrest was due to workers not being able to spend their higher wages (!) on better accommodation, especially as so many families were divided because of their inability to find any accommodation to house a united family. Failure to investigate, failure of private enterprise, failure of local authorities to appreciate their full powers, rapacity of owners for compensation, antiquated methods of arbitration, absence of a definite basis for compensation and the high prices of land are amongst the obstacles to reform cited by the Commission.

The Commission's primary recommendation was that for immediate and practical purposes, over a period of 14 years (with an opportunity of revision at the end of 7 years) the State should assume full responsibility for providing working class housing, and should operate through municipalities, on which the obligation to provide accommodation should be made statutory. Thus was created the basis of housing policy that determined the main thrust of urban development in Scotland for the central years of the twentieth century.

The first step was the Housing, Town Planning, etc (Scotland) Act 1919, which enabled central government to subsidise municipal housing schemes for the first time by providing both powers and resources. Glasgow – like other municipalities – embraced the Government initiative enthusiastically, and the Corporation's Works Department (the predecessor of the Direct Labour Organisation) was set up in 1920 to carry out the work. A major increase in municipal housing followed the Housing (Financial Provisions) Act 1924 which was known as the Wheatley Act after the Glasgow MP who was the Housing Minister in the first Labour Government.

And so the inter-war period is dominated by local authorities building new housing estates. In some, the tenemental form continued as new walk up flats with bathrooms and kitchens. Much of the new housing was inspired by the Garden Cities movement. In Glasgow, the 'garden suburbs' of Knightswood, Riddrie and Mosspark are the result of this approach to urban design in the 1920s and 1930s

The Garden Cities movement goes back to the turn of the century when Ebenezer Howard developed the first 'Garden City' at Letchworth in England. Garden cities were to be planned, self-contained communities surrounded by parkland with balanced

Knightswood

areas of residences, industry and agriculture. Once again, public health was at the centre of this movement. Separating the pollution, noise and smells of industry from housing and access to green space would – it was argued – improve the health of the nation.

One of the important Scottish voices in favour of the Garden City approach was Patrick Geddes, not an architect, but a botanist. And yet he was undoubtedly one of the fathers of Town Planning. Although his name is not as well known as the international architects like Le Corbusier (and certainly not as well recognised in his own native Scotland), he has had a huge influence on the thinking of many in the architectural profession. He supported the Garden Cities; he was critical of the new tenements for working class people that were still being built before the First World War – citing tenements round the Singer Factory in Clydebank, and around the breweries at Duddingston in Edinburgh – arguing that what should be built were Garden Cities. He was critical of the delays in getting the first Scottish Garden City established at Rosyth.

Geddes advocated Garden Cities in his 1915 book, *Cities in Evolution*, as an antidote to overcrowding; the separation of home from grimy workplaces; an opportunity for people to be close to nature; of 'social co-operation and effective good will'. And of course they required proper town planning. But he stressed that such suburban development depends on good transportation systems, and emphasised that the development of suburban railways, trams and buses would allow for the growth of suburbia. It is this vision

29

which was attractive. Geddes would have been pleased to see some of the inter-war housing estates in Scotland, with their broad avenues, low rise housing set in individual gardens and with plenty of open space. One suspects that he would have been less pleased with how suburbia has turned out with its dependence on the private car and often without the 'chumminess' of Geddes' vision of the Garden City. Many of our suburbs lack the cooperativeness and what Jane Jacobs would later describe as the 'eyes in the street' approach of mixed communities.

However, Geddes advocated a different approach to existing neighbourhoods. He was not convinced of the Parisian approach which he described as 'monotonous' and 'pompous'. He was also concerned about the impact of large scale redevelopment on the lives of local people. In Edinburgh he developed the concept of 'conservative surgery' – originally a medical approach to removing only the incurable parts rather than whole limbs. Geddes promoted the concept for historical neighbourhoods like the Edinburgh Old Town. Where possible, modernisation and improvement of the existing buildings should be undertaken, minimising the unnecessary destruction of the built heritage, avoiding significant disruption to the residents, and respecting the social and cultural traditions of the community. In the 1890s he had put his thoughts into action by moving into the Old Town. He began to improve it, and then organised the neighbours into communal action – not just undertaking physical improvements, but developing social programmes.

Geddes was not just about improving the conditions of the poor. He clearly believed that socially and economically mixed communities were essential for the wellbeing of the city – and to encourage the better off to come back he developed Ramsay Gardens as co-operative flats to persuade University professors back to the Old Town at the top of the Royal Mile in Edinburgh, Ramsay Gardens contains flats of a mixture of sizes, recognising that household needs are different. Ramsay Gardens was near to his visionary Outlook Tower – an educational approach to an understanding of Edinburgh, its region, and significantly its relation to the world at large.

Nor was Geddes simply concerned with the social and built environment. He was a botanist by training and at heart. The

Distant view of Camera Obscura atop Patrick Geddes' Outlook Tower built amongst the squalorr of Edinburgh's Old Town

John Reiach

31

Environment Society was set up to improve and renew the Old Town environment. This was the organisation that grew to be the Edinburgh Social Union – reflecting Geddes' own view that environment and social concerns go hand in hand – Work/Folk/ Place. The botanist advocated the Garden as a place where education through hand, heart and eye could be achieved. Small sites were identified where local people – particularly young people – created gardens. We would now call his approach 'sustainable development'. And all this in the last decade of the nineteenth century.

Geddes' vision of 'conservative surgery' was not tried in Glasgow, although there had been calls to improve existing buildings. In 1891, the Church of Scotland published 'The Report of a Commission of the Presbytery of Glasgow on the Housing of the Poor'. This advocated the establishment of an association to purchase and reconstruct existing tenements which were insanitary and in disrepair. The report had no official status and was ignored by the authorities. The city was pushing forward with large scale redevelopment – modernising and replacing the old. In 1909 the first statutory provisions for town planning were introduced; the general aims were concerned with securing proper sanitary conditions, amenity and organisation of land use. These were mainly concerned with new land for development. And, as often happens, modernity regards its immediate predecessor architecture as poor, unacceptable and even something to be reviled (as is currently the case with buildings of the 1960s and 1970s!). So the Victorian buildings – particularly tenements – were ignored and regarded as buildings to be replaced in due course.

However grand the vision, there was a limit to how much could be changed in the twenty years between the wars. Many of the old tenemental areas – often at the heart of the old burghs (like Govan and Partick) that had been gradually absorbed into Glasgow at the end of the nineteenth and early twentieth centuries – were largely untouched by redevelopment. New housing schemes had been inserted, but the core of these former burghs remained. The seeds of future housing problems were also sown. Not all houses were built to the Garden City standard. The Garden suburbs were primarily designed for skilled and white collar workers. Cheaper developments, including poorer quality tenements, were used for slum clearance. They attracted a social stigma early in their life, from which some never recovered. The social stratification of the poor was reflected in housing allocation policy.

Although rent restrictions under the 1915 Act were removed at the end of the war, further unrest – including more strikes – saw new rent restrictions in 1920. One consequence of this legislation was a lack of investment – arguably because the expectation was that these tenements too would have a short life and would be replaced. There was also a prevailing political attitude among Labour councils that no public money should go into the hands of the private landlord. From the landlords' perspective there was no financial return to be made from the tenement. The polarisation between tenant and private landlord left both in a state of limbo.

And to understand what happens next to the tenement, we need a diversion into post Second World War Glasgow.

Moss Heights

Queen Elizabeth
Court – the
Gorbals flats
designed by Sir
Basil Spence and
now demolished

3. After the Second World War – a new society?

'The people. . . deserve and must be assured a happier future than faced so many of them after the last war'

Labour Party Manifesto 1945

IN 1945 the war had been won, and the challenge was to win the peace. Rationing, bread queues, crumbling transport infrastructure and poor housing characterised the challenge. Change was about to take place. A typical British 'revolution' occurred in 1945 when what might be described as 'the people's party' (Labour) won the election. It was committed to creating a better, fairer society, through the 'Welfare State'. However, there was a consensual element to the welfare state – two of the architects came from other parties – Beveridge, who chaired the committee that produced the report recommending widespread reform to the system of social welfare, was a Liberal, while Butler was the Conservative that pushed through the 1944 Education Act. The new Government quickly moved to create the National Health Service (NHS), set up National Insurance, free secondary education, nationalisation of transportation and utilities. All of this brought together a centrally organised state. The approach to city development reflects this centralisation.

The big clients were to be the public sector, and the public sector would also drive change forward despite the problems that emerged. This was a confident public sector that knew what it wanted and thought it knew what was best for everyone. There was no public participation as we might now understand it. It was, however, a period of huge public information campaigns, and a significant amount of consultation; a lot of which has survived in the form of film.

The Government had a very difficult inheritance; it was not simply about a post Second World War reconstruction. The inter-war period had left its mark – depression, unemployment, labour unrest, and the start of a programme to provide better working class housing (by new build) meant there was no question of a return to pre-war 'business as usual'.

In his 1976 study of Glasgow, *The Upas Tree*, Sydney Checkland, calls his chapter on 1945-75 'The Faltering Economy'. In it he explains that the Upas tree of heavy engineering had killed or discouraged the growth of other industries of a more modern kind beneath its massive and intertwined branches. Checkland argues that, in economic terms, Glasgow had died before the First World War. The economy based on heavy engineering industries had been kept alive by two World Wars and between the wars no-one realised that the recession in Glasgow was any different to anywhere else. At the end of the war Glasgow had been overtaken by other places which had modernised, and the markets had changed. For example Glasgow was still building steam engines long after anybody else, and by the time diesel locomotives were being built many of the competitors in other cities and countries had established more successful designs.

Housing conditions were particularly poor. Despite the interwar housing programmes, there remained far too many working class tenements that lacked investment and too many families had to share an outside toilet. Serious overcrowding continued, both within individual houses and within neighbourhoods. So a major priority was the provision of better housing – with higher space standards, bathrooms, and more external open space.

A typical Govan backcourt in 1970

Various aspects of the welfare state were interlocked. The housing programme was also seen as part of improving the health of the nation along with improvements brought about by the NHS. The challenge was how to tackle the amount of tuberculosis, polio, and rickets – much higher in Glasgow and the west of Scotland compared with the rest of the UK – and much of it related to poverty and bad housing conditions. So the 1950s would see major campaigns to eradicate disease through mass vaccination and immunisation; for example in Glasgow there was a mass radiography campaign as part of a plan to reduce the city's tuberculosis rate. New housing with lower densities and more green space was also seen by the City's municipality as a contribution to curing the ills of what was one of the 'sickest cities in Europe'.

Much of what was happening in urban development in Scotland had been prefigured in the 1938 Empire Exhibition held in Bellahouston Park in Glasgow. The exhibition had created visions of a new Scotland, of new places, new architecture and of a new society. The ambition was even stronger after a seven year gap. Young architects (and engineers and planners) came back from the war determined to create a better Britain. The attitude was summed up as 'we have to improve the quality of life for ordinary people. We want to create places where people want to live. Architecture will serve a social purpose'.

This was not simply to be 'a land fit for heroes' as had been the slogan at the end of the First World War. There was a belief that a better physical environment would create better people; that behaviour is caused entirely by the characteristics of the environment. It was a belief that came to be known as 'Architectural Determinism' and was not until the mid 1960s that it was seriously challenged. Subsequent social research has discredited the belief, but there still remain elements within the approach to urban regeneration by some within the architectural and planning professions.

In some ways the gap between 1938 and 1945 was immaterial. During the war there had been significant preparation work for the post-war reconstruction of Scotland. The approach to regional and national planning had been developed with the clear aim of improving the conditions of the working class. In Glasgow in 1945 the waiting list for council houses was approximately 90,000 families, or a quarter of a million people. The debate was about how this scale of challenge was to be met. To achieve the objectives, densities were to be reduced. There was a general feeling that the tenements that housed low income private rented tenants were slums. Slums must be removed. The state must provide housing for the working class and therefore the slum tenements must be demolished. The professionals – planners and architects – would create the new utopia, to match the new approach that would be taken to employment, health and transport.

Economic diversification was to take place, so planners and architects developed industrial estates like Hillington, alongside new opportunities for old industries like the expansion by the National Coal Board in Ayrshire and in Fife. Other parts of the country were to benefit from the engineering (and design) achievements of the nationalised North of Scotland Hydro-Electric Board.

In the post-war story of Scotland, Glasgow is the critical place. It was the second city of the Empire. The city dominated the urban developments that were to be undertaken. It dominated the economic life of Scotland. And it dominated all the statistics in terms of ill health, squalid housing, and high densities. At the end of the war, it had a population of over one million. Of these 700,000 people were living on 1800 acres at a density of over 400 per acre, with some as high as 700 per acre – one of the highest population densities in Europe.

Immediately after 1945, there was what could be dubbed the 'battle of Glasgow'. In reality it was the debate about how Glasgow should be developed, and it took place between the Government and the City Corporation. It had a profound impact on the kind of city that was to be developed during the 1950s and the consequences are still with us today.

In brief, the story is this. During the war the Government commissioned Sir Patrick Abercrombie (with Robert Grieve and Robert Matthew as part of the team) to develop the Clyde Valley Regional Plan, which was published in 1946. The process involved much research, analysis and consultation. As a regional plan it covered almost half the population of Scotland, and followed some of the principles that had been set out in the Royal Commission for the Distribution of the Industrial Population in 1940 (the Barlow Commission) which advocated that urban growth be restrained by the adoption of a positive policy of developing new and expanding towns. The key issue which in many ways was going to dominate thinking over the next twenty years was that Glasgow's population should be reduced and dispersed. The Clyde Valley report suggested that approximately 250,000–300,000 people should be moved away from the city.

However Glasgow was still a proud city and had its own idea. In 1944 the City's Engineer, Robert Bruce, produced his plan in what became known as the Bruce Report. This was the city's answer to the Clyde Valley Regional Plan. The city effectively rejected the Clyde Valley plan by proposing to concentrate its population within the city. And it wanted to go further. It proposed to create a whole new central business district. The plan was to flatten the city centre including the Art School, the City Chambers and various other buildings of historic and architectural value, and create a new civic centre, with a broad boulevard connecting North and South railway stations. All of this was to be a single design with the aim of creating a coherently planned city. A ring road was to encircle the new city centre. The Bruce Plan was followed by a transport plan. Instead of the population being reduced, the city would create high density estates, much of which would be modelled on Le Corbusier's Ville Radieuse. (Once again the continental European influence!) This was removing the past and creating a new architectural order which reflected the new kind of society.

Glasgow pressed on and created its four big peripheral estates – Castlemilk, Easterhouse, Drumchapel and Pollok. These estates had to be built according to local by-laws which included that they should be dry areas – in other words they had no pubs. They were mostly welcomed; people loved them when they first went there. They provided large houses – no overcrowding; they had bathrooms and kitchens; and plenty of external green space. Moss Heights was the first multi-storey development, designed in 1946 very close to the site of the Empire Exhibition but not opened until 1953. From then on, 'multis' would be a key part of the solution (and would be encouraged by Government grants for the next twenty years).

Eventually a compromise was agreed between Glasgow and the Scottish Office. And as is often the case with compromises, it was not the best of either proposal. The ring road was built (or at least half of it); there was significant overspill to new towns and expanding towns (to begin with overspill was related to employment opportunities, but later simply overspill); lower densities; plot ratios defined for central business districts which in the Glasgow context meant no higher than seven storeys – and that defined the kind of architecture that was going to be built in the city centre. But the city centre was not to be flattened.

Driving the ring road round the city centre involved large scale demolition of mainly very poor quality tenements. At the same time a series of 29 Comprehensive Development Areas (CDA) were to be developed, each planned to regenerate an area through demolishing all but a very few buildings and replacing them with new – all of which were to be publicly owned. This particularly applied to housing and schools and, because many of the houses were to be in flatted developments with ground floor shops, even the shops were to be publicly owned.

The public sector would comprise the Corporation or the Government's own 'housing association' – Scottish Special Housing Association (SSHA). SSHA had been set up under Act of Parliament in 1937 to be the Government's direct housing arm – and although called a housing association its constitutional position was quite unlike what are now housing associations. It had direct access to government funding.

For the CDA programme, Glasgow hired the best architects of the day. Basil Spence, Robert Matthew and others were commissioned. This was Glasgow being a good client and demanding nothing but the best in architecture. And of course being at the forefront of modernity. The idea that any of the 'working class' tenements should be improved was political anathema.

Queen Elizabeth Court, the blocks of flats designed by Basil Spence (now demolished) in many ways represents the challenges, the issues, and the debate about the architecture of the period, particularly for the public. The two buildings that formed the high rise blocks might have looked like magnificent sculptures – but they proved difficult to live in. Rain leaked into the building, the lifts kept breaking down, as did the social structures. Many see 'modern architecture' in that light, see it as de-humanising, and the perpetrators as egotistically forcing an alien architecture onto an unsuspecting public. But many of these are the same people who admired Tait's Tower at the Empire Exhibition, who voted for the new brave world after the war and rejected their Victorian inheritance.

It is important to put Queen Elizabeth Court into the context of the huge achievements made over the twenty years between 1945 and 1965. In that period, more and more people had been better housed in terms of space standards. More and more people had bathrooms. Fewer and fewer people were living in a one or two-roomed house. There was a reduction in population density, more access to green space and there had been a redistribution of the population. The car had become a means of transport for the many, and not just the few. The nation's health had improved dramatically – illnesses that were common at the end of the war had been virtually eliminated, and the hospitals were beginning to be upgraded or replaced. In economic terms, jobs had been created and people had more disposable income. Large parts of the visions that people had in 1945 of a better society had been accomplished. Like many visions, the new architecture and the new society had created other, often unforeseen, problems. Utopia had not arrived. Nor had all the tenements been demolished. By 1970, we still had a long way to go – the CDAs had really only started, and thousands of people were still living in appalling conditions. And the assumption that everything should be demolished was beginning to be challenged.

But before looking at that challenge, it is worth reminding ourselves of Sidney Checkland's conclusion, in 1976, about the thirty years of Glasgow's post-war reshaping. He writes in *The Upas Tree*:

The rebuilding of Glasgow has not been the outcome of blind brutalism. Much consultation and discussion went into many aspects of so vast an undertaking. The research base was often elaborate and careful, but as there's never enough partly because many of the questions asked do not become apparent until a commitment has been made. There was too the need in order that situations be made manageable to reduce them to overriding formulae. The three most important of these were the setting of plot ratios for the central business district, the establishment of densities for redevelopment areas and the setting of the overspill figure. Politicians and planners are certainly fair

41

targets for public criticism but their job of urban renewal should be seen as totality and over time.

By the mid-1960s, there was a growing public dissatisfaction with the kind of new places being created. In Glasgow, the dream of better places (in the peripheral estates) exemplified in Doreen's song in Tony Roper's play *The Steamie* had been overtaken in 1967 by Adam McNaughton's 'Skyscraper Wean' the last verse of which included the phrase 'we're goan tae march on George's Square demanding civil rights'. And it was not just people in the peripheral estates that were unhappy. Those being re-housed back into the CDAs were finding that the utopias which had been designed with such enthusiasm had their problems – of damp houses, of social structures breaking down and, like the peripheral estates, devoid of variety of shopping and meeting places.

The built environment was once again a political issue; this time the architecture and planning professions were not in the lead – they were regarded as the problem rather than the solution. This was compounded by the collapse of the Ronan Point tower block in London in 1968, with architects getting the blame for poor construction, for encouraging policies that created 'soulless' estates. They were not totally to blame – politicians had pushed for numbers of houses to be built at the lowest possible cost and had ignored concerns about quality.

For the planning and architecture professions, some of the post-war confidence had been shaken. However, enough had been left to question whether there was something missing in the urban regeneration approach. And at the same time inner city communities and those in peripheral estates were becoming unhappy about the places that were being built for them. There were real pressures for change.

4. Glasgow rediscovers its past

'The past. . . a store of possibilities awaiting disclosure and translation into the language of today.'

Søren Kirkegaard

IT IS HARD to believe today that as recently as the mid 1960s Glasgow's architectural heritage was seriously under threat. While the threat of the total destruction and redevelopment of the city centre as proposed in the Bruce Plan had receded, the plans for the inner ring road and the growing CDA programme were to lead to large swathes of the city being cleared of its nineteenth century buildings.

Few mourned the passing of the Victorian buildings. Glasgow was undergoing what was then described as the largest urban reconstruction programme in Europe. The ring road was the twentieth century equivalent of the railways; this time the Corporation was committed to re-housing people – mainly in the peripheral estates. What was being swept away was Victorian – seen by many as ugly and overblown. It was also dirty – blackened by

Rev David Orr

St Enoch's station entrance and hotel – demolished in 1977. This picture shows how smoke-blackened Glasgow buildings were in the 1960s. One of Glasgow's saddest losses before the city realised the benefits of conservation – and stone cleaning

decades of soot. And they reminded people about the rather grim industrial past. There may have been grumblings about the quality of the new estates, but few argued against the demolition of the tenements.

However Glasgow was about to re-evaluate its past. As before, the architectural profession was to play a key role. While the Corporation was driving forward the redevelopment, some people began to be concerned about how some of the best buildings and places were being threatened. The New Glasgow Society was formed in 1965 as a Civic Society to highlight public interest in the built and natural environment and to draw attention to Glasgow's historic architecture. The founding group included bookseller Robert Clow, architect Geoff Jarvis and Professor Freddie Feilden from Strathclyde University's Architecture Department. They held public meetings in threatened buildings and mobilised action and demonstrations. Civic Societies had been promoted since 1957 in England; the New Glasgow Society was one of the first in Scotland. In 1967, the Scottish Civic Trust was formed as 'a coordinator of action for individuals and groups across Scotland; a focus for debate and criticism'. The work of the Civic Societies gave impetus to the creation of the Civic Amenities Act of 1967, giving statutory force to the designation of conservation areas. The national mood was changing.

As often happens, it takes an outsider to tell us what we really need to value. Glasgow Corporation commissioned the distinguished architect and town planner Lord Esher to carry out a study of the city, following a similar exercise he had carried out in York. His report 'Conservation in Glasgow' was published in 1971, and formed the basis for the first group of conservation areas in the city in 1972.

And change in attitude towards tenements?

While the middle classes campaigned for the conservation of the high quality architectural jewels in the city centre and the West End, very few people campaigned to retain the working class tenements. Most tenements suffered from a lack of maintenance, and shared toilets were still the norm. The conditions which many families had to endure were intolerable. Not just the flats; the war effort had taken away the dividing railings within backcourts making control of space impossible and they had deteriorated into swampy rat infested areas.

Investment had been negligible. Landlords and factors blamed rent controls while the subsidised public sector's low rents set tenants' expectations for equally low rents in the private rented sector. And there was worse. The misery of those forced to live in the slums was exploited by some – not all – private landlords. The name of Rachmann will forever be associated with immoral private renting practices in England. Scotland had its equivalents. The lower end of the private rented sector was therefore seen by all parties as having had its day. And just as the private sector should go, so should the tenement – to be replaced by high quality public sector houses.

There had been attempts since the 1930s to improve the private sector tenement. In the 1930s, the Glasgow Property Owners and Factors Association attempted upgrading at 388 Tollcross Road when the Association bought the building from the then owner and plans were drawn up. However the war intervened and their proposals were not implemented. From time to time during the 1950s there were calls for area rehabilitation as an alternative to demolition and rebuilding, but they fell on deaf ears.

Implementation of the legislation that followed the Royal Commission in 1919 had concentrated on new building for general needs; any provisions for replacement and improving 'unfit housing' were not widely used. The term 'clearance area' did not enter the statute book until 1930 and thereafter serious slum clearance began – but not improvement.

The war time work of the Government's Scottish Housing Advisory Committee (SHAC) is best known for its 1944 report *Planning our New Homes*, which recognising the shortages of skills and materials, set out recommendations and model plans which were to have a major impact on post-war housing developments. Less well known is that in 1939 it had suggested that a programme of improvement might be a desirable supplement to a new house building programme. During the war much thought was given to an improvement policy, but this was mainly confined to agricultural and mining cottages. Tenements were considered too difficult from a technical and administrative perspective.

In 1947 SHAC published the report *Modernising our Homes* (the McTaggart Report). Douglas Robertson, who has been researching planning in the post-war period, points out that the McTaggart Report:

> represented a distillation of ideas and experiences about home improvement and went on to provide a strong and reasoned justification for the adoption of a large publicly-funded improvement programme to ensure those not immediately involved in the post-war reconstruction did not have to suffer the indignity of living in inadequate housing. A complete policy framework was provided involving the introduction of improvement grants, with attractive subsidy levels, facilities to allow rent increases and strong compulsory powers.

The only policy that flowed from *Modernising our Homes* was the introduction in 1949, of the first improvement grants. However, there was very little take up. 1954 saw steps to resume action on older housing on a large scale – local authorities were to produce programmes of slum clearance. Between 1955 and 1965, Glasgow demolished 32,000 houses – mainly flats in Victorian tenements. In 'Reshaping a City', Tom Brennan in 1959 argued for the improvement of tenements, proposing that a city-sponsored housing association could 'purchase, recondition and manage houses' should the private landlord be unwilling to do so. Again, the voice fell on deaf ears – indeed it had been virtually forgotten when tenement improvement was to start in earnest years later.

Two particular developments led to changes in policy – one by Government (national and local) and the other by voluntary action. Both are important in the changes that are to take place as they intertwine to enable the development of tenement rehabilitation.

Firstly, Government action. By 1965, public sector housing production was reaching a peak of over 34,000 new units per year. However, large numbers of sub-standard housing still remained. Estimates of how many varied – as did the interpretation of what was meant by 'sub-standard' or 'unfit'. In 1964 the Corporation of Glasgow commissioned a housing survey of the city. A year later the Government set up a Committee of Enquiry relating to the whole of Scotland. Both studies were carried out by J B (Barry) Cullingworth from the University of Glasgow. The Committee reported to the Government in 1967 (the Cullingworth Report). The outcome was a recognition that, amongst other things, in Glasgow one in four houses lacked sole use of a WC. There are some clear similarities between the recommendations of the Cullingworth Report and the McTaggart report nearly twenty years earlier.

Cullingworth proposed first a 'Satisfactory Standard' – as a policy target, and a 'Tolerable Standard'. Thus the letters BTS came into housing policy jargon – Below Tolerable Standard. Houses falling below it would be subject to statutory action – either for demolition or improvement. These would be houses that failed on one or more of nine points: structural stability, dampness, lighting, ventilation and heating, water supply, provision of sink, sole use of a WC, drainage, cooking facilities and access to outbuildings.

While demolition and replacement was regarded as the normal approach, the scale of the problem identified was such that the Committee also recommended that two distinct types of improvement – full improvement to meet the 'Satisfactory Standard', and lesser improvement to make unfit houses tolerable to live in until they could be demolished.

The Cullingworth report noted that although improvement grants had been available to private owners since 1959, few had been applied for. As David Whitham has explained in his contribution to *Architectural Heritage XXII* the reasons they were given included the attitude of local authorities (little or no encouragement was given); the amount of grant available (discretionary grants by the local authority were limited to 50% or £500 (about £10,000 in 2012); 'standard grants' for basic amenities – both required an expected life of fifteen years); and the difficulty of improving tenement flats. The Government responded by setting up an internal professional improvements team which carried out detailed studies into the technical challenges of improving tenements and into the standards that should be sought. The tide was beginning to turn.

The Cullingworth report led to new legislation in the form of the Housing (Scotland) Act 1969. Besides the adoption of the 'Tolerable Standard', this emphasised the need to plan for 'Housing Treatment Areas' (HTA) of substandard housing, by replacement, improvement or a mixture of both, and placed a duty on every local authority to ensure that BTS houses be closed, demolished or brought up to standard in a reasonable time. The challenge was set down, and supported by technical advice in the form of Scottish Housing Handbook 'Slum Clearance and Improvements' – Bulletin 2.

Secondly, the potential for upgrading was being investigated by voluntary bodies around the time that the BBC showed *Cathy Come Home* in 1966 which highlighted the plight of homeless families. The film coincided with the launch of the housing charity Shelter and in turn it supported a group of recently formed Church sponsored housing associations. The constitutions of the new associations declarted that these would be charities or Industrial and Provident Society organisations.

In the Gorbals in Glasgow in 1965 a young Rev. Richard Holloway (to become Primus of the Episcopal Church of Scotland and a future chair of the Scottish Arts Council) was horrified by the conditions in which people he worked alongside were forced to live but yet recognised the intrinsic value of the tenements. He was one of a group who established Christian Action (Glasgow) Housing Association with complementary associations in Edinburgh and Greenock. The Association was not initially concerned with the improvement of whole tenements, but opportunistically acquired and improved individual flats to house homeless people. It exploited the relatively unused improvement grant arrangements, installed bathrooms with ingenuity and made the flats habitable and available to let at affordable rents.

The aftermath of the Great Storm of 1968

It could be said that the real event that changed the attitudes towards working class tenements was the Great Storm of January 1968. 'God got fed up and blew the roofs off the city'. On the night of January 14/15, the city was hit by hurricane winds. Roofs which had not been maintained properly for years were swept off, twenty people were killed, and the extent of the damage became a national issue. Temporary repairs had to be carried out and the Corporation of Glasgow established a Storm Damage Section to coordinate the city's response to the storm. The Storm Damage Centre was developed from the Civil Defence Section and therefore took a military style management approach – output focused and well organised. It was highly regarded for the way it tackled the scale of the problem. It was therefore well suited to being converted into the House Improvement and Clearance Section (HICS) of the Town

Clerk's office as part of the Glasgow's response to the 1969 Act.

And it introduces one of the most important figures into the story
– Theo Crombie – who will become increasingly important as the
story unfolds. He was a highly personable and pragmatic man and
one of the most effective and organised council officers. Without
Theo Crombie, Glasgow's tenements may not have been improved.
With the HICS, Glasgow's administrative infrastructure had been
established. The storm concentrated minds on the need for
improvement and repair action, since it was quite clear that many
tenements would have to survive for many years. Delivering an
improvement programme was going to need all of Theo's skills.

Theo Crombie

Despite the reputation the Corporation of Glasgow had for acting
independently of the Government (indeed of believing that it alone
could solve the city's problems), Theo worked closely with two
civil servants to ensure that both local and national government
would tackle the sub-tolerable problem in Glasgow in a coordinated
approach. David Whitham was a senior architect in the Scottish
Development Department (SDD) and was the leader of the team
that developed the survey techniques that helped to assess the
country's housing stock as part of the Government's response to
the Cullingworth report. Peter McKinlay was an Assistant Principal
in the same department. This was a partnership that was to see
another senior member of the Development Department's Architectural staff – John Girling – seconded to the HICS. In 1970 a joint
report from SDD, HICS and the Corporation's Planning Department
led to the drawing up of a joint ten year programme for 100,000
houses for the city. This target would be achieved partly by building
more houses within the city boundaries, some overspill and –
important to our story – 10,000 houses in tenements to be
improved.

The technical issue of getting bathrooms into nineteenth century
tenements had still to be solved. Enter again the University of
Strathclyde and its Architecture Department. Peter Robinson was
an undergraduate student whose final year study in 1969 set out
to test the Cullingworth proposals by showing what might be
possible by way of improvements to tenement buildings – whole
buildings, not the one-off solutions which Christian Action Housing
Association was forced to do. His study concluded with a demonstr-
ation flat, owned by Christian Action, in Gourlay Street showing

with a mock-up how a bathroom could be fitted into a bed recess. The mock-up attracted attention from the Corporation, the Government, and from the Ideal Standard Co Ltd who with the University's Centre for Industrial Innovation looked at the possibility of prefabricating fibreglass bathrooms. A prototype was exhibited and installed in an improved house. However, the standard 6ft x 4ft bedrecess proved not to be quite so standard, and the project was not developed.

On graduating, Peter joined the civil service and worked with David Whitham and Christian Action Housing Association on what was proposed to be a pilot project in Oatlands in Glasgow. Unfortunately it did not proceed, but it allowed further development of the ideas of plumbing stack, repairs and basic environmental improvements.

The question that remained was – how was improvement to be carried out? Since the tenements were in private ownership – and by this time in multiple ownership because many people had been buying their flats – could improvement be done by the owners themselves as hoped for by the 1969 Act – in other words voluntary improvement? Could the Corporation work with the owners, or should the Corporation promote the use of the Compulsory Purchase Order (CPO) powers that the Act bestowed on them and undertake the work itself? One part of the Corporation – interestingly the architects – believed that the answer was to use CPO powers and improve the buildings as if they were new developments. But in another part of Glasgow Corporation there were other approaches that were being tested. The issue was one of public participation in the planning process. And this was to have an impact on the way the future was to go – even although – as we shall see, the CPO route was also to be tried.

Public participation in planning

The 1960s was a period of dramatic changes in Western societies. After the austerity of the late 1940s and early 50s, there was a desire for more freedom in personal and community life. It was the decade in which we reached for the stars and landed on the moon. The decade of the pill and of the Beatles. The decade of the Vietnam War and the challenges to that war. The decade in which mass marches and civil rights agitation led to desegregation in the USA.

The decade in which Britain lost most of its empire – some of it peacefully, some after local civil unrest. The 60s could therefore also be described as a decade of protest. From students in France to riots in USA it was a decade in which the traditional authority of political systems was being challenged.

In Britain, Harold Wilson won the 1964 election for the Labour Party after 13 years of Tory rule, which he was to repeat again in 1966. By 1969, the pound had been devalued and the long period of Northern Irish Troubles had begun. In Glasgow, the decade ended with a grouping of Progressive Unionists ousting the Labour Party which had run the city since 1952. This group ran the city, leaving the Labour Party to re-establish itself and return in 1972.

In urban planning in Scotland, the right of the individual to have a say in the planning of his environment was written into the Town and Country Planning (Scotland) Act 1947 – but it was basically in the form of objections. By the late 1960s public demand for greater involvement had led to planning legislation by way of both the Civic Amenities Act 1967 and the Town and Country Planning (Scotland) Act 1969 (and its English 1968 equivalent) that incorporated statutory requirements for publicity and participation in the development process. The Government set up the Skeffington Committee 'to report on the best methods, including publicity of securing the participation of the public at the formative stage in the making of development plans for their area'. Skeffington defined participation as 'the act of sharing in the formulation of policies and proposals. . . participation involves doing as well as talking and there will be full participation only where the public are able to take an active part throughout the plan making process'. Brave words! They started a process – techniques of explaining, of involving, of sharing information and above all sharing power are still being widely used today.

One of the members of the Skeffington Committee was Charles Murdoch, Depute Town Clerk (Planning) of Glasgow Corporation. His involvement ensured that Glasgow, in its most recent Comprehensive Development Area (CDA), would try out some new ways of participation. The CDA chosen was Govan.

But before moving our story into Govan, there is one further piece of the background jigsaw which would see the developing interest in tenement improvement combined with the growth of public participation. Not that it was planned that way. Skeffington was a starting point for another unusual undergraduate thesis at Strathclyde University, following that of Peter Robinson. In their final year, architecture students are required to undertake a year-long project – normally a complex design such as an airport or an opera house. The intention is that before being released into the real world, the student can demonstrate an ability to design.

This is where the story gets personal. As explained in the preface, I was less interested in designing buildings and more in whether the powerlessness of ordinary people to impact on their environment could be changed. And so when it came to my final year thesis, I persuaded the University that I should look at 'Design Participation'. I was fortunate that the Department was willing to look at something even more unusual than Peter's project – it was unlikely that I would even produce a set of drawings! Two tutors were allocated to the project – Jim Johnson, an architect who was himself involved in social issues concerning architecture and particularly housing. He had been Peter's tutor, and had also played a part in a campaign against the City Architect's design for a new concert hall. The second tutor was Sean Damer a sociologist who had been studying 'Wine Alley' – an inter-war slum clearance project in Govan, and helped to ground my fanciful ideas in academic rigour!

Jim Johnson of Strathclyde University demonstrating to architecture students

There was the usual period of investigation and of writing; looking at growth of public participation in the UK, at the Model Cities Program in the USA, at community organising by people like Saul Alinsky of Chicago, and Jane Jacobs. The reorganisation of local government was under debate at the time, and it and the question of political participation was central to the study. Some architectural thesis!

Two important visits helped shape what was to come. The Shelter Neighbourhood Action Project (SNAP) in Liverpool 8 was a locally based technical and advice service in a Housing Improvement Area (the English equivalent of a Housing Treatment Area) funded by Shelter as a pilot with the hope that it would ginger Liverpool Corporation into developing similar organisations across the city. At the same time, in Wales, the Welsh Office, led by their Chief Architect Jim Grove, was developing a participatory approach to Improvement Areas in the Valleys – organising local community groups and supporting them through the local authorities – 'What is required here is a concentrated treatment of a small geographical area by all departments'. Both projects were concerned with house improvement (of two storey houses) and the environment around the houses.

At the end of the investigatory period, there was then a question of whether a 'live' project could be undertaken. Three possible projects were considered which would allow some of the lessons from the research could be tested. Three options were considered in parts of Glasgow – working with a youth group to design and convert an old disused church into a youth club (for which there would have been a set of drawings!); an urban planning exercise for the centre of Springburn (not really followed up); and something with the New Govan Society which had been set up in response to the Corporation's public participation process in the Govan Comprehensive Development Area. One idea, however, stood out above the rest. Peter Robinson had shown a technical solution to tenement improvement; what I was interested in was how it could be implemented – and done in such a way that would involve the owners and tenants. Independently, in 1968 a Strathclyde planning student, Douglas Bailey, had carried out a study on 'Twilight Areas' – on the potential improvement of tenements in economic and social terms.

The timing was right – there was a growing interest in tenement improvement, public participation was the new credo in the planning world, and a 'live' project might be possible. Would the New Govan Society be interested?

The Govan Ferry

Govan Cross

5. Govan and
the New Govan Society

'What is the point of cities built without the people's
wisdom?'   Bertold Brecht

MY DIARY for 28 December 1969 reads: '10.30 meet the Rev.
David Orr, at the Pearce Institute, Govan'. In retrospect this
was one of the most important meetings of my life! I recall it clearly.
I had been to Govan before – or at least had been through it. In my
teenage years, I went to a club in Langside College, and cycled
there from Maryhill across the ferry – first the vehicular ferry before
the Clyde Tunnel was built and thereafter on the pedestrian ferry
from Partick. Those were the days when Govan was connected by
car ferry to the north side of the Clyde, and it was a crossroads
place. By 1969, the cross roads had moved – the Clyde Tunnel
took traffic away from the centre of the district – it had been 'by-
passed'. But it was still connected to Glasgow by the magic of the
Subway that rattled its way under the Clyde and although electrified
in 1935 still smelt of the 'tarry rope' that had pulled the cars round
from its opening as the world's third underground railway in 1896.

I climbed up from Govan Cross Station and into what was still a
busy shopping area, with a variety of shops serving a range of
customers. In Harmony Row, for example, there was a Ladies'
Milliner to which 'ladies' from all over the South Side of Glasgow
came to buy their posh hats. Govan was a melting pot. It was proud
working class community, in which the sights, sounds and smells
of heavy engineering that was shipbuilding and its associated work
were never far away.

The Pearce Institute (known to many simply as the P.I.) is a
magnificent Edwardian building at Govan Cross – at the heart of
the old burgh. Designed by one of the leading architects of his day,
Sir Rowan Anderson, the P.I. had been gifted by Lady Dinah Pearce
as a lasting memorial to her husband Sir William Pearce MP –
Govan's first MP (and a Tory). He had made his money as a
shipbuilder and his statue stands opposite the P.I., affectionately

Chris Fletcher

The PEARCE INSTITUTE GOVAN   C. K. Fletcher   1977

The Pearce Institute

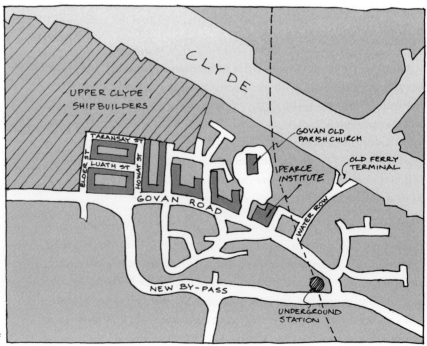

CLYDE

UPPER CLYDE
SHIPBUILDERS

TARANSAY ST
ELDER ST
LUATH ST
HOWAT ST

GOVAN ROAD

GOVAN OLD
PARISH CHURCH

PEARCE
INSTITUTE

OLD FERRY
TERMINAL

WATER ROW

NEW BY-PASS

UNDERGROUND
STATION

Govan town centre

known as 'the Black Man'. The P.I. was designed to provide educational, recreational, social and religious facilities for the working men and girls (*sic*) of Govan. It developed to be Govan's Community Centre.

Lady Pearce quickly established a Trust to manage the building (including the Provost of Govan, the Principal of the University of Glasgow, and the Clerk of the Presbytery of Glasgow). Soon afterwards she agreed to the Trustees entrusting the day-to-day management of the building to the Kirk Session of Govan Old. The building therefore acted as halls for Govan Old Parish Church as well as a base for a wide variety of community facilities.

The P.I. was the last of the munificence by the shipyard owners to the Burgh. In 1912, the Burgh of Govan was absorbed into the City of Glasgow. It

The Black Man (statue of Sir William Pearce) at Govan Fair time

had only been an independent burgh since 1864. By 1912 it was the fifth largest burgh in Scotland. Even in 1970 there were many people who commented that amalgamation day was the blackest day in the history of this proud community, with its very strong sense of place. Over the last 40/50 years Govan has suffered with the decline of shipbuilding; the regeneration plan which was launched with such high hopes in the 1960s has taken so much longer than expected to be delivered. Govan has developed an unfair reputation – partly through the television series *Rab C Nesbitt*. At last – albeit slowly it is recovering from the image as it is now being reconnected to the city by river as well as underground. Immediately opposite is the new Riverside Museum, and a ferry service has been re-established. The designation of the mediaeval historic core as a Conservation area along with subsequent environmental improvements is part of a slow recovery. Govan has a long history. Bounded on the north by the river, on the south and east by the M8 and on the west by Renfrew it has feeling of isolation and of independence.

Over a millennium ago, Govan was a Royal and religious centre. Govan Old Parish Church stands on one of the oldest Christian sites in western Scotland. It has been in continuous use since approximately 565 AD. The church houses one of the largest and

Govan Old Parish
Church

best collections of early historic sculpture, including what is regarded as a royal sarcophagus. Govan's location on the river made it an important crossing point and recent research has shown that it was a significant weaving community with global connections, and a highly desirable place to live. Govan is of course best known as a shipbuilding community – growing from the early nineteenth century. Robert Napier who ran Govan's oldest shipyard from 1841 is regarded as the father of Clyde shipbuilding. It was a centre of innovation and its products sailed the seven seas.

In 1970, however, Govan was no longer the place it had been. Shipyards were closing. Harland and Wolff at the centre of the town had closed in 1963; Fairfield's and other yards faced bankruptcy. In 1968 – at the same time as the Comprehensive Development Area was launched – the Government created Upper Clyde Shipbuilders (UCS). But it was not just the shipyards that were on their last legs. Behind the apparently solid walls of the tenements were flats in poor condition, with the majority of families still sharing a toilet, with backcourts that were a mixture of an unorthodox adventure playground for children and a playground for rats.

Rev David Orr

Govan Shipbuilders Ltd (established 1972 after the 'work in') – better known as Fairfield's shipyard looking across the Clyde

Community facilities were also old and tired – schools needing renewing, public baths remodelling, and even the cinemas could do with a makeover. And the densities were very high. It felt like a place where no investment had been made in the infrastructure for a long time – it was living on borrowed time. The CDA was a lifeline.

The New Govan Society

David Orr was the Minister of Govan Old Parish Church and, as a consequence, chairman of the Pearce Institute Trustees. He had made a conscious decision to live in the P.I., and therefore to be fully integrated into the life of the community.

Govan Old Parish Church had been a central feature of the community for a millennium. In more recent times, its fame has come from the inter-war period, when George MacLeod was minister. Horrified by the impact of unemployment, he tried to find new ways of relating the church to ordinary people. In the process he was to found the Iona Community with its commitment to justice and peace. At that time many of its minister members worked in inner city parishes or new parishes in housing estates. David Orr was one of them.

I went to see David Orr, not as P.I. chairman nor as minister nor as a member of the Iona Community, but as chairman of the New Govan Society. I was looking for a partner to work with, and I had heard that the Society had led the community representation during the public participation process that had been used when Glasgow Corporation developed its Govan CDA plans in 1968. The CDA plans had been approved with significant amendments proposed by the Society, including that of the first houses to be built on the banks of the Clyde. I saw this as an organisation that might be interested in testing out some ideas about public participation during the redevelopment period.

What was this New Govan Society and where did it come from? Its origins lie in the fourteenth centenary celebrations of Govan Old Parish Church in 1965, at the conclusion of which David Orr wrote in his church magazine (incidentally a major resource of information, which in the twenty first century would have been described as a blog):

Rev David Orr

> I myself am in no doubt that these exciting times are an age of new reformation for the church and a worthwhile congregation is one which sees that it has a part to play in this. We have the additional incentive of a new Govan in prospect. Having managed to modernise the Institute, having remembered and honoured our great past in our fourteenth centenary year, and having sought to embellish our fine church building by means of 'operation 1400', we are now at the stage where we must turn round and look to the future, when we must become outward-looking and learn how better to be the church in the new Govan and the new world.

He went on to explain that the Kirk Session had set up 'a political group':

> This arises from the responsibility of a parish church to be concerned about the life of the parish in which it is set, and from the repeated exhortations of successive General Assemblies that church members must play their full part in the political life of their communities and of the nation.

A New Govan Society Sunday afternoon walkabout

This was the secd that led to a meeting of councillors, local people and other church leaders in February 1968 – convened by David Orr. 'A steering committee had been set up to take the necessary steps to this beginning and to ensure that the people of Govan might share fully in the re-planning of their community.'

The New Govan Society (NGS) was formed on 26th April 1968. David Orr was appointed its first (and eventually its only) chairman. Vice chairman was Mrs. Logan, the secretary of the Govan Ward committee; secretary and treasurer was Mr. Campbell, the headmaster of Govan High (this was a tradition that was to be followed by his two successors – Harry Wylie and Bob Lennie). The committee included Councillor Dan Docherty (Labour), Councillor Derek Neilson (Conservative), Willie McShane (the chairman of the Fairfield Ward Committee – the forerunner of today's Community Councils), Mr Hall from Govan Traders Ltd., and Canon Cusack from St. Saviours Roman Catholic Church. A complete mixture of 'community leaders'. Such was the optimism of the initial meeting that 2,000 membership cards were printed. Some 300 people attended the inaugural public meeting, and by October 1968 the New Govan Society had 495 members.

It was a good time to set up such an organisation. The Corporation of Glasgow had decided that Govan, as a major Comprehensive Development Area, should be a test bed for 'public participation' under the new Skeffington proposals. The Scottish Civic Trust was encouraging the establishment of Civic Societies, and the New Govan Society was recognised very quickly by the Corporation as an organisation with which it could do business. When the plans for the New Govan were exhibited, as the Corporation's first essay into public participation, they were of course exhibited at the Pearce Institute (for three weeks from 20 August 1968 and from 2pm to 9pm), and the exhibition was part manned by the NGS. The Society arranged a series of explanatory meetings and, through this process of working closely with the Corporation, succeeded in making changes to the plan.

The Corporation's own documentation, reviewing the speed with which the proposals were approved, noted in an undated report:

> This Society (New Govan Society) was given a certain credibility by the planners and the Council because it seemed to be talking for a number of groups and had met with no opposition from the three Ward Committees or the Councillors in the area. Fairfield Ward Committee say that they have been 'identified with the New Govan Society since that body came into being. The Ward Committee has also been represented at meetings with the planners'.

The report noted the comments of the reporter (to the public inquiry into the CDA plans) on how useful had been the collaboråation between the department (Planning Department) and the Society:

> The New Govan Society was formed and collaborated closely with the Planning Department, which has freely acknowledged that, for example, the Riverside plans in place of the former shipyard derived their major ideas and initiatives from the people of Govan, in particular that that strip should be residential rather than industrial. This may not be so successful in areas with less community spirit than Govan. I believe that the process could be carried further. . .

The New Govan Society was important to the future progress of redevelopment in Glasgow. Partick, Maryhill and Springburn took up the model where public participation in the CDA programme became a way of life for planning in the 1970s.

But once the Comprehensive Development Area plans were approved, there were further things for the Society to do. It encouraged tenants' associations, campaigned for a proper shopping centre, set up the Govan Area Resource Centre, and gave evidence on the role of community councils at the time of local government reorganisation. What it had not expected was to become involved with a student proposal in public participation (and one that would also lead to the Society becoming part of a pioneering programme of tenement improvement). That is what I put to David Orr. His response was to invite me to submit a formal proposal to the next committee meeting in January 1970.

The proposal was 'for a scheme for public participation in the detail planning of your area which allows maximum scope for local initiative, within the constraints of the Govan CDA'. Although the CDA proposals had been approved by the Secretary of State, there were areas that were not going to be redeveloped until the final phases of the CDA. At that time the estimate was around fifteen years to complete the redevelopment. I suggested that we jointly look at a tenemental area in the last phase; use a 'survey before plan' (Patrick Geddes) approach to start, then set out alternative solutions to the problems identified. Public participation techniques would be used and developed to decide what action could or should be taken. There may even be a physical solution – possibly a back-court improvement as an indication of collective action.

I also explained my interest in participation, suggesting that unlike a redevelopment area, the future population of an improvement area can be easily identified, thereby overcoming a major difficulty encountered in the statutory process of public participation in planning. Area improvement, went the argument, is one of the functions of local government most suited to decentralisation. And I was sure that people in neighbourhoods were capable of carrying out improvements themselves if they are encouraged to plan their own environment and are provided with some technical and administrative assistance. The basic rule – if you want people to participate, start where they are.

964 Govan Road –
the Tenement
Improvement Project (TIP)
office (and the author's
flat!) was on the second
floor in the centre (no bay
windows)

I suggested that if the Society was interested in me working with them, then I would move into the area and have an accessible office; that the Society would help to guide my work and help with introductions to the neighbourhood (through public meetings). It was clear what benefit I was likely to get – a degree; but what was in it for the New Govan Society? The answer was – exploring a new role for Civic Societies like the NGS!

The Society's committee accepted the challenge and set up a 'Task Force' of three people to work with me – Willie McShane; Barbara MacDougall and Celia Nichol. At the same time, Jim Hewitson, a member of the NGS Committee and a partner with David Watson, the locally based house factor, identified a flat for me to rent at 964 Govan Road. It was on the second floor, a middle flat, room and kitchen (i.e. two rooms) with an inside toilet. (I was to discover later that that the better quality houses in terms of sanitation provision were on the main road, with those further away being the ones with shared toilets). One room was to be the office. I moved in, and meetings of the Task Force began.

The Task Force met weekly, looking at the issues and discussing how we would involve the wider community. Willie was the local backcourt sweeper (he worked for the Cleansing Department of the Corporation) and as chair of the Fairfield Ward Committee he had strong political connections. He was the younger brother of Harry McShane, known as one of the 'Red Clydesiders', who lived with Willie and Willie's wife. Willie was one of those Glaswegians of his generation for whom education was important. Despite leaving school at 14 he had a huge thirst for knowledge and was one of the best read – I suspect that he had read most of the 'heavy books' in the local library. Barbara was a tenant in the study area and was to become a leading member of the housing association. Celia represented the churches and was to emigrate not long after.

(above, left) The study area backed onto Fairfield's shipyard

(above, right) Taransay Street – dominated by the shipyard wall

I had suggested a particular tenement area for our study area, between Govan Old Parish Church and Upper Clyde Shipbuilders (Fairfield's), and between Govan Road and the yard – the yard was on two sides! It had been identified as being in the final phase of the CDA plans – to be the site of a further education college. Redevelopment was planned for the final phase of the CDA – expected to be in fifteen years time. There were 749 houses in the study area, of which 612 were below the statutory tolerable standard (BTS). It was a typical 'twilight area' in its population structure, multiple ownership and low incomes. It offered cheap accommodation, low cost shopping and good public transport. 30% of the houses were owner-occupied; 2.6% were privately let on a furnished basis with the majority being let unfurnished.

An early public meeting in the Pearce Institute chaired by Willie McShane introduced the Task Force in their particular role – not just me. The Task Force discussed methods of public participation – including explaining architectural drawings to a lay audience through models and other techniques now regarded as standard (until 'fly-through' computer imaging was available!). We looked at the processes for improvement. Newsletters explaining the project and a proposed survey were delivered. Our progress and ideas were regularly reported by the local weekly newspaper – the

Elder Street

Govan Press – whose owner, Harry McNab, was also a member of the New Govan Society.

A three pronged survey approach was adopted:

- general survey – to provide statistical data – carried out by the Task Force with support by me

- social survey (very small sample) – on demographics, attitudes – carried out by me with support from sociologist Sean Damer

- house and building survey – by myself with some support from another Strathclyde student David Martin, later to become Conservation Officer at Glasgow City Council. (He also built models of the Treatment Area that helped explain the proposals)

Further public meetings took place – including a critical one when Peter Robinson came and explained about house improvements. What therefore emerged from both the survey and the public meetings was not a backcourt improvement proposal (that was to wait until later in the story), but an interest in having a bathroom in their homes. The Task Force looked at the possibility of short life improvement – with a life expectancy of ten/fifteen years. This was in line with the Cullingworth report, and would involve low capital cost and higher maintenance costs to manage the repair work and to ensure that the housing conditions were maintained at a reasonable level. The ten/fifteen year time period would allow a child to grow up with a bathroom inside his/her home. Thereafter, according to the CDA plan, the tenements would be demolished to make way for the proposed college.

The survey results showed that the area was suitable for improvement; that there was some interest in having housing improved, and that it would be physically possible. The six month undergraduate project was over. But it proved not to be the end, but in Churchill's words, not even the beginning of the end, but the end of the beginning.

Would you want to play in this backcourt?

Luath Street – a play street!

6. Annie's loo

'Life's a drudge with an outside cludge,
but an inside loo is a joy for you!'
          Fairfield Residents Association Govan Fair Banner

WHILE LIVING in Govan and working with the New Govan Society Task Force, I also watched ships being built. To a student architect, watching these great pieces of architectural engineering slowly but methodically rise from the ground and then slide into the river was fascinating. I wanted to sail on them. At the end of the six month period I graduated. But I did not go to sea. Professor Tom Markus offered me a Social Sciences Research Council studentship to develop the ideas that were being worked up with the Task Force, and to submit for a second degree. The Tenement Improvement Project (unfondly known as TIP) was born. So I stayed.

Before TIP really got underway, there was a diversion and a learning experience. Glasgow Corporation, with the enactment of the Housing (Scotland) Act 1969 had approved in principle its first Housing Treatment Area in August 1969. The Old Swan, in the Pollokshaws district, was at the edge of another Comprehensive Development Area, an important 'entrance' corner to the city from the south-west. The Corporation proposed to undertake the task of carrying out the improvement work itself. Their approach was to use the City Architect's Department to prepare a set of plans and put them to the residents. The 'consultation' took the form of 'take it or leave it'. And the same techniques as were being used in the CDAs were proposed – take ownership of all the houses (mainly through Compulsory Purchase Orders (CPO), re-house all the people (who could then be Corporation tenants or take their compensation and move elsewhere), strip out the buildings and completely refurbish.

Not all of the owners agreed. Margo and Douglas Weir headed up a residents' group and made contact in mid-1970 with a couple

The Old Swan in 2012

of planning students and me. We agreed to help – and it would be an opportunity to put into practice the 'community engagement and empowering' theories that had formed much of the 'Design Participation' study. So we helped arrange close meetings; set up a residents' committee; held surgeries advising people how they could go about changing the Corporation's mind and how they could undertake the improvements themselves.

The Corporation arranged a series of public meetings at which we 'activists' argued with councillors – telling them that they were there to represent the will of the people and not the Corporation. Strong stuff! We lobbied for and were granted a meeting with the Housing Committee which turned out to be confrontational. The residents' committee was primed to take control of the meeting. In the event, the Housing Committee chairman said that he was willing to meet the residents – but only the residents. He insisted that the 'advisors' (us) had to withdraw. Game, set and match to the Corporation when the unity of the residents began to fall apart.

The Corporation's preferred scheme went ahead, although the Weirs and some of their neighbours were moved into a couple of tenements that were excised from the CPO and which were not sub-tolerable. It would take until 1973 before the CPO for the Old Swan was approved and firms invited to tender for pilot improvement work. The Old Swan was a very valuable lesson in power brokering and community engagement. Another tack had to be developed.

For me it was back to Govan to 'think again'. This time to see if working with, rather than against, the Corporation might bring more success.

As we have already noted, with the passing of the 1969 Act, the Corporation had set up the Housing Improvement and Clearance Section (HICS) – in reality the private sector housing department. HICS was headed up by Theo Crombie and he had arrived at the post at precisely the right time. And he had not been involved with the Old Swan. He listened to the ideas that the New Govan Society (NGS) Task Force, supported by the local councillors and ward committees, had been working up. And he was willing to give us a chance (although probably in private thought that we were mad).

In February 1971 the first TIP report on the potential for rehabilitation in the area was completed. A sample survey showed clearly that people wanted to stay, wanted the area improved and were willing to pay towards it. It was physically possible; 612 out of 749 houses were below the tolerable standard (BTS). To deliver the improvements would require the Corporation to declare a Housing Treatment Area (and the TIP survey could be used as evidence in that declaration); the University to establish an Improvement Office; the creation of a housing association; and a pilot improvement project to be carried out as a both a test and a show house.

In May 1971 Willie Ford, an SNP Councillor for Govan arrived at my door. He told me that John and Annie Gibbons at 2/1, 10 Luath Street wanted their house to be improved. They had persuaded their neighbours in the same side of their building to join in. However the occupant of the top flat was a tenant. Fortunately, her landlord, although not prepared to take part, agreed that the water, soil and vent pipes could go though his flat, provide we made good any damage to his tenant's flat. We had a vertical stack with three bathrooms one on top of the other, and the ventilation pipes through the top flat. The technical challenge had been overcome in a multiple ownership tenement.

And then disaster! John Gibbons, who worked in Upper Clyde Shipbuilders, came home on June 15 with a redundancy notice – the shipyard was closing. Everything was put on ice as the Upper

DUCT FOR SERVICES WATER, VENTING

VERTICAL SOIL STACK

BED RECESS CONVERTED INTO BATHROOM

MANHOLE CONNECTION IN CLOSE (SOMETIMES DRAINS GO STRAIGHT TO FRONT OR BACK)

Drawing of vertical stack

ASSIST

Upper Clyde Shipbuilders
Gate

Clyde Shipbuilders 'Work-In' set about saving the yard from closure.
The 'Work In' is often seen as a 'bottom up' approach to dealing
with economic and social issues – an alternative to the traditional
approach of mass strikes. It caught the Government off balance. In
some ways, the approach that TIP/NGS was taking was equally
designed to be different – and maybe even catch the Corporation
off balance?

While the plans for Annie's loo were put on hold, in the same
month the Corporation designated the Govan (Taransay Street)
Housing Treatment Area in one part of the study area – 216 flats,
covering a whole block bounded by Taransay Street, Howat Street,
Luath Street and Elder Street. Thanks to Theo Crombie, the
Corporation also agreed – unlike in the Old Swan – to refrain from
taking powers to enable them to promote a Compulsory Purchase
Order to see if voluntary improvement was possible.

In some ways this delay proved to be quite fortuitous. We had
realised that the delivery of a rolling improvement programme
would require more than just a stack of bathrooms. The process
would require a number of elements which all had to be available
at the same time. So while supporting the 'Work-In' by joining in

the local marches, the various elements of the package that was to deliver the rehabilitation programme were put together.

A housing association

First was the creation of the Central Govan Housing Association (CGHA) – what was to become the first of a new kind of housing association – community based. We had set it up earlier in 1971. CGHA was not the first association in Glasgow; mention has already been made of Christian Action (Glasgow) Housing Association. There were others, but most of these tended to provide housing for middle income groups in the form of co-ownership housing which, in return for a financial investment, the occupant received a share of the increase in value of the property when he or she moved on.

It had been clear for some time that not every owner in the Treatment Area would be either willing to improve or would be financially able to do so. While tenements had been built on the basis of rental properties, many landlord owners had decided that the income was so poor that they sold off their flats on an individual basis rather than continuing to rent them. So for a number of owner-occupiers, buying a house was the only way they could get a home. This was very different to the cultural shift that was to occur twenty years later with Right-to-Buy. Sub tolerable houses were not able to attract a home loan from a building society, a bank or through the local authority's own home loan scheme. Purchasing a BTS flat meant buying on a variation of hire purchase – deposit and instalments. And the companies which offered financial assistance in this way did not always operate 'to the highest ethical standards'. For some 'home-owners' (in quotation marks because they did not become the owner until the final payment had been made – thus the variation on hire purchase) the thought of being able to sell their house and rent it back improved from a reputable landlord was a very attractive proposition.

TIP and the New Govan Society had discussions with both Christian Action Housing Association (already building up a stock of 'one-off' flats across the city) and with Bill Law, the Scottish Officer of the National Federation of Housing Societies (NFHS). As a result we decided that a housing association was the most sensible vehicle to be able to acquire and improve houses which the owners did not want to improve themselves. Its role was to be a supportive one, a safety net to ensure that all the houses could be improved. We could have invited Christian Action or another association to undertake the role. However, the project had been started on the basis of public participation. All of the existing associations operated on a self selecting membership policy, and it was felt that an association that reflected the participatory ethos would be better. Had the plan been to acquire all the houses, then a co-operative might have been the answer. Instead, it was felt that membership should be open to everyone within the Treatment area and its environs. And so the concept of the community based association was formed.

A small amendment to the model rules published by the NFHS ensured that all residents – tenants and owners – had an automatic right to be members and therefore stand and/or vote for the committee. However, someone had to set the ball rolling and the founding committee which registered the Association with the Registrar of Friendly Societies in February 1971 came from the New Govan Society. It was led by James F Stephen, chairman of Alexander Stephen of Linthouse (shipbuilders), who became the Association's first chairman, with two other Govan business people – Harry McNab, the proprietor of the local paper (the *Govan Press*), and Jim Hewitson, a partner in the local house factor (David Watson) which was also to handle the management of houses being bought by the Association. Barbara McDougall, David Orr, and Jim Johnson were also recruited as members. They were joined by Fiona Fisher, who was the Youth Worker in the Pearce Institute, and lived in Howat Street and, to begin with, therefore was the only member who lived (as a tenant) in the Treatment Area. I acted as Secretary.

The involvement of so many business people was intentional – there were no subsidy arrangements. It was therefore hoped (and subsequently proved right) that some support from the business community would be required to get funding to top up the improvement grants available from the Corporation. Thanks to Christian Action HA, the Corporation had set up a system of providing loans to upgrade houses to the tolerable standard, and Central Govan HA was to take advantage of this in its early years.

Govan Housing Association collection

Jim Stephen (left), the first chairman of Central Govan Housing Association photographed in 1989 with George Irvine, the first Chief Executive of Scottish Homes at the opening of the environmental improvements around the Treatment Area

A residents association

The second organisation was the Fairfield Residents Association. This was created in October 1971 – at a time when it appeared that the 'Work-In' was beginning to be effective (although far from over). The launch meeting was chaired by Councillor Robert McClement thus ensuring that there was local political support – this was not to be a 'pressure group'. Unlike the Old Swan, the delivery of improvements in the Govan (Taransay Street) Housing Treatment Area was to be a collaborative effort between the residents and their Corporation. The Residents Association was a traditional community organisation with representatives from each close (tenement), and like many community organisations was run by a group of women, even although it had a male chairman (Peter Lewis). Sheila O'Halloran became its energetic Secretary who would drive the organisation forward. The Committee met weekly; with the help of what was to be known as ASSIST, it published a regular newsletter and information sheets on improvement processes and grants; and held public meetings – a role which it took over from the New Govan Society. It became the main vehicle for marketing improvement – including a float at the annual Govan Fair.

Rev David Orr

Sheila O'Halloran, Secretary of Fairfield Residents Association

An architectural service

The third part of the organisational structure was developing TIP as a properly organised and constituted architectural and technical advice service. It was reborn, at the same time as the Residents Association was established, as ASSIST – a formal University of Strathclyde Department of Architecture and Building Science Research Unit, with Jim Johnson as Project Director. I was appointed Project Architect. (The name was chosen because the Department already had a Research unit called ABACUS. ASSIST started as Architects and Students Strathclyde Improvement Service to Tenements. That was quickly forgotten and has simply been known thereafter as ASSIST!) We aimed for an office with a street frontage, and it was clear that delivering an improvement service could not be done simply by one post graduate student and a part-time secretary being paid from the overdraft on the postgraduate grant. (The first commercial investor in the project was the Royal Bank of Scotland which provided the overdraft!). Although

Three key Fairfield Residents Assocation members – Annie Gibbons (the Annie of Annie's Loo) with Effie McGeorge (left) and Carrie McLean (right)

the Government was interested in what was going on, no finance was forthcoming. David Whitham promised that 'a grant would be available when hot water came out of a tap'. We would have to struggle on until then. So a shop front would take some time to arrive, and one room of my two-room flat remained the office. Margo Weir from the Old Swan volunteered to provide an advice service – it had become known that we knew a few things about planning and the CDA. One of Margo's first successes was arranging for a sink to be lowered so that a lady well under five feet in height could wash her dishes without having to stand on a box. Such was the variety of the ASSISTance given! Strathclyde University architecture students Archie Provan and Graham Houston became part-time team members.

In setting up ASSIST, the formal proposal put to the University and funders in August 1971 was that Govan would be:

> . . . a model for a locally-based improvement service offering technical, professional and administrative aid to resident's associations and to individuals. . . to complement the work of the Corporation in the House Improvement and Clearance Section; to demonstrate that voluntary improvement is practical; and thereafter to persuade the Corporation to set up its own local service.

> It could be argued that the local authority should offer this kind of service but it is felt that not until the reform of local government in Scotland in 1975 will there be an opportunity for this kind of service to be put into action. . . To avoid 'means-testing' the service will be free. The future cost of such as service should be rate borne.

> The primary aim will be to improve tenement houses. There are still so many unknown factors that it is difficult to predict with any confidence a turnover or rate of improvements that could be achieved. A secondary aim will be to compare the rate and results of voluntary improvement with Glasgow Corporation's preferred technique using compulsory purchase. ASSIST will try to evolve improvement techniques which will minimise the expense and inconvenience to residents. . . it must not be forgotten that improvement is essentially a holding operation. Improved dwellings can at the most have a life

of 20-25 years. After this time structural decay will be accelerating and social change will probably render the dwellings even less desirable that they are today. . . people cannot be left in such poor conditions for another 15 years.

It is the intention to record and evaluate all the work of ASSIST and to publish when results warrant such action.'

We may not have had a plan at the beginning, but by the time ASSIST was set up we had a vision of a network of local authority offices. Also important was the academic underpinning – this was to be 'Action Research' with the intention of influencing policy.

A contractual system

Fourthly, if we were going to improve houses on any scale (other than one-off flats), a new form of contractual system would have to be developed. Help with contracting and pricing was required, and a quantity surveyor was added to the team. Theo Crombie introduced us to Ian Sloan of Armour and Partners. He had played an important part in the storm damage work, and was to be the mastermind behind a unique contracting system that, in David Whitham's words 'treated the installation of a bathroom like the purchase of a TV'.

As Peter Robinson had demonstrated, Glasgow tenements involved much standardisation; for example the bed-recess. We were not proposing a complete refurbishment, but upgrading. So a set of standard parts were designed – e.g. a range of bathrooms that could fit into the bed-recesses using a standardised plumbing stack; a range of kitchen units that could be used to upgrade the old kitchen sink, and basic repair items such as replacement window cills. Ian Sloan then produced a 'Master Document' that set out the specification for each bathroom and kitchen type and added repair elements for each house and close. All these referred back to the standard drawings that were at A4 size, thus creating a manageable sized book. We did consider computerisation of the Master Document – but this was long before we had compact computers. Instead it was typewritten.

The drawings and the specifications were submitted for Building Warrant approval and discussed with the House Improvement and

Clearance Section, during which agreement was reached about grant eligibility. Next, Ian Sloan negotiated prices first with one contractor, but later when the programme was fully operational with three contractors. The prices were confirmed for a fixed term and were then agreed with the Corporation for grant purposes. This meant that the ASSIST team was able to present the house owner with the range of bathrooms and kitchens, and tell them exactly how much it would cost; irrespective of contractor. The owner was therefore able to sign up knowing how much it was going to cost them. Having liaised with local banks ASSIST was able to tell them how much a loan repayment would be. The Corporation also made loans available – including to unemployed householders which was a significant breakthrough. Although loans to buy a BTS house were almost impossible to obtain, loans for improvement were available because the house would no longer be sub-tolerable. So installing a bathroom was like buying a TV – either outright or with a loan.

The contract between the owner and the contractor was a two page document which listed a series of codes that referred back to the Master Document. The form was signed by the owner both as his/her application for grant and the building contract. A copy was sent to the Corporation (as the grant application form), to the contractor (as instructions on the work to be done), to the owner and to ASSIST (for the records). ASSIST used the same information to make application for Building Warrant. The contractor, HICS and ASSIST all had copies of the Master Document. The process was quick, simple and relatively un-bureaucratic.

The first contractor to be brought into the team was again one who had proved himself during the storm damage period. George Finlay and Partners was a small Glasgow east end multi-skilled contractor with plumbers and joiners and plasterers on his staff. The firm acted as main contractor for the electrician and other trades. Because the prices were fixed and transparent, Finlays became part of the planning team – indeed part of the wider partnership.

A re-housing programme

There was one last piece of the jigsaw before the programme could get fully underway. There were 216 flats in the Treatment Area; normally three flats to a floor. The largest was of two rooms; a

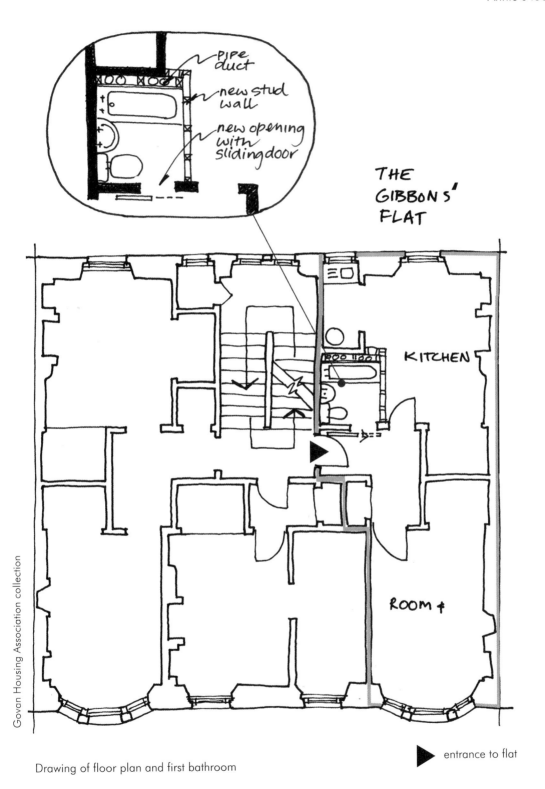

pipe duct

new stud wall

new opening with sliding door

THE GIBBONS' FLAT

KITCHEN

ROOM 4

Drawing of floor plan and first bathroom

▶ entrance to flat

THE
GOVAN PRESS

A WEEKLY NEWSPAPER FOR
GOVAN, KINNING PARK, PLANTATION, IBROX,
CARDONALD, MOSSPARK, POLLOK, CROOKSTON,
HILLINGTON, PENILEE, BELLAHOUSTON, DUMBRECK,
LINTHOUSE, DRUMOYNE AND CRAIGTON

ESTABLISHED 1878

ESTABLISHED 187

94th Year—No. 41

POSTAGE OF THIS PAPER IN UNITED
KINGDOM, 2½p

Friday, October 8, 1971

number of centre flats were 'single end'. Some families had indicated that they would have liked a larger flat; while others wanted to move away from Govan. Negotiations with the Corporation's Housing Department led to a voluntary re-housing scheme giving those who wanted to leave priority. It also meant that in many cases larger flats of up to four rooms could be created – with the leaving owner selling to his/her neighbour at District Valuer's valuation – and the building works cost included in the contract.

With the team in place and with the prospect that the immediate crisis in Fairfield Shipyard might be resolved thanks to the 'Work-In', John and Annie Gibbons' application was formally submitted in October 1971. The *Govan Press* followed each move, starting with photos of Annie handing in her grant application appearing on its front page and thus building up interest locally.

The Residents Association carried out another, but more detailed survey of residents in November 1971 – obtaining information on attitudes towards improvement (including for the first time environmental improvements to the common backcourt), willingness to work with neighbours, and identifying who wanted to stay or leave. This was submitted to the Corporation as evidence of voluntary improvement.

With Annie's grant application approved, George Finlay and Partners carried out the improvement work to the eastern half of 10 Luath Street. It went according to plan. It took 10 days. The Gibbons and their neighbours lived in their flats throughout the process. The pipe duct was delicately inserted through the top floor

Govan Residents Want Action

Govan Residents Want Action

A Govan houswife made history this week when she handed Glasgow Corporation an application form. She was asking them for a grant to make improvements to her home... and is almost certain to be the first person in the Govan Redevelopment Scheme to do so.

Original cutting from 1971

A Govan housewife made history this week when he handed Glasgow Corporation an application form. She was asking them for a grant to make improvements to her home... and is almost certain to be the first person in the Govan redevelopment Scheme to do so.

For the past 17 years Mrs Annie Gibbons, her husband and family have lived in their room and kitchen at 10 Luath Street, with no hot water or inside toilet.

When the Corporation announced in their redevelopment plan for Govan that the houses in Luath Street and the surrounding area would not be demolished for at least another 15 years, she decided something had to be done.

HELP

She sought the help of architectural students from Strathclyde University who had been working in the area and together they worked out aplan whereby a bathroom – containing a bath, wash hand basin, w.c. and sink with hot water – could be built into a bed recess.

Now, if Mrs Gibbons' application for a grant is successul, work could start within the next few weeks.

Said Mrs Gibbons: "It's terrible in this day and age to be living in a house that has an outside toilet."

She added: "If I get the grant it will work out a lot cheaper than a new house and I'll have all the facilities."

FOLLOWING

And it looks as though many of Mrs Gibbons' neighbours – in Elder Street, Howat Street, Taransay Street as well as Luath Street – will do likewise.

At a meeting in the Pearce Institute on Monday night they met and listened to Mr Raymond Young, a Strathclyde University architect and Mr Robert McClement, Labour Councillor for the Fairfield Ward.

Said Mr McClement: "At the present moment we can and should condemn 6,000 houses in Glasgow. Of course we cannot build that number. We have a problem. We can help this if we slow down the rate of decay.

"It will take time to rebuild and in this time we think something should be done to improve the existing houses."

Something has already been done, for a team of Strathclyde University students led by Raymond Young has carried out a survey in a block of houses bounded by Elder Street/TaransayStreet/Luath Street Howat Street.

They found that many had an outside toilet, none had a bath and most of the back courts were in poor condition.

They survey showed that people asked first for an inside toilet and bath, and seven out of 10 said they would be willing to pay part of the cost or, in the case of a tenant, pay an increase in rent.

TREATMENT AREA

Said Mr Young: "On June 10 the Corporation declared the area as a housing treatment area.

"This means that grants are now available to improve things like houses and back courts," he added.

"It would cost between £700 – £800 to have a bathroom installed in a house similar to that of Mrs Gibbons," Mr Young revealed, "and with a 75 per cent grant that would leave about £125 – £200 for the householder to pay."

Loans are also available from Glasgow Corporation to assist house-holders to pay their share. "If the owner borrows this money over a period of time it could be paid back at about 50p per week," added Mr Young.

To advise tenants how to go about getting a bathroom installed Strathclyde University are to provide a free profession service in the P.I. every Monday between 6.30 p.m. – 8.00 p.m. It will be called ASSIST and its aim will be to help owners and tenants get a grant and generally smooth out snags.

The feeling of the meeting was that as individuals they lacked power. So seven of the tenants have formed the committee of a Govan Residents' Association and will work together with the students.

flat, carefully protecting the tenant's wallpaper and fittings, so that there was a vertical pipe run and stack.

On 10th February 1972 the Grand Opening was carried out by Councillor Pat Lally, the chairman of the Corporation's Clearance and Rehabilitation Committee. His own ward was that of Oatlands – where Peter Robinson and Christian Action Housing Association had tried but had been unable to carry out an improvement programme. Pat Lally was not known for his enthusiasm for rehabilitation, but like most people favoured the 'Clearance' bit of his committee's title. However, in the presence of senior Corporation officials, the press, TV and, most importantly, a house full of excited local residents, he declared the bathroom open by cutting a ribbon, having declined the 'Clochmerle' invitation. Annie Gibbons also declined to be photographed in the bath! But photographs were taken (not by us, but by the *Govan Press*) and STV carried the story in the news. Over the next few weeks over 300 people – including some very senior government officials – climbed those stairs at 10 Luath Street to view the remarkable phenomenon of 'Annie's Loo'.

300 View Mrs. Gibbons' House

ANNIE GIBBONS could rightly cliaim to be Govan's most popular housewife … for she's had no less than 300 visitors to her home this week.

They've been visiting Annie's second-storey room-and-kitchen flat at 10 Luath Street to see her new bathroom which was converted from a bed recess.

It's been open-house at Annie's ever since last Thursday when the first of her neighbours began queueing outside the 70-year-old red sandstone tenement.

Among the first visitors was Councillor Pat Lally, convenor of Glasgow Corporation housing sub-committee on clearance and rehabilitation.

HEARTENING

He said how heartening it was to see a tenement, scheduled for short life, being improved and given a new lease of life.

"Usually," he said, "tenements in the last 10 years of life deteriorate rapidly. Now these improvements will stop that happening."

And Mrs. Gibbons' neighbours shared his sentiments.

"I think it's wonderful," said one. "It's money well spent."

"It's been the best thing since sliced bread," added another. "I can't wait to get mine done."

In all, 120 houses are expected to have the conversion done on their bathrooms, provided the Corporation grant an extension to the present six months given to carry out the scheme.

Mrs. Gibbons house is the first to be modernised within the Govan/Taransay Street Housing Treatment Area and was only made possible by "ASSIST", a voluntary house improvement advisory service run by Strathclyde University under the leadershp of Raymond Young.

The university team were able to draw up the plans and take on the responsibility of the legal and architectural problems.

GREAT NEED

Said Raymond: "There was obviously a great need for an agency like "Assist" to be available to come in and give all the families living up a close the guidance and help they need to reach those agreements which allow for an improvement of this kind to go ahead."

Up until now, Glasgow Corporation, because of the problems involved, have so far favoured a procedure whereby they acquire all houses within a Housing treatment Area in order to improve them. Occupiers would then be evacuated during reconstruction work under an agreement which allows them to re-occupy the houses as Corporation tenants.

All the work on Mrs. Gibbons' houses, which was undertaken by the building firm of George Finlay and Partners, was carried out while the family lived in the houses.

Mr. J. H. Johnson, Senior Lecturer in the University's Department of Architecture and Building Science, said: "The three houses in Luath Street, which we have treated independently, are the first to be completed in any HTA with Glasgow – and Taransay Street HTA is one of the latest designated.

"Of course, we fully acknowledge that the time taken to complete the improvement of ALL the houses in the area is the true measure that must be applied, but it is perhaps significant that the "Assist" group has already been approached with a view to helping to improve another 135 houses in the vicinity."

VOLUNTARY

The University team has been working in the Govan flats for 18 months applying lessons learned during an earlier conversion experimentally undertaken in 1969 in Springburn. A principal objective during the work was to demonstrate that voluntary improvement is completely practicable for owner-occupers and tenants provided they are able to enlist a locally-based service for technical and administrative help.

The experience the team has gained in Govan has prompted the plan to establish "Assist" as an organisation equipped to provide such assistance.

Added Mr. Johnson: "Our intention is to set up an office in Govan where advice and assistance will be available.

"The Wates Foundation of London, a charitable trust, is willing to fund half the £19,000 which it is estimated will be needed to operate "Assist" for two years – provided the balance can be raised at this end. We are confident we can do this."

FOOTNOTE:
Glasgow Corporation housing sub-committee decided at a meeting this week to recommend to the Housing Committee that a further six months be granted to the Taransay HTA so that the other houses can be improved. It is thought unlikely there will any oppositon to this.

Govan Fair float

Tommy Barrie (left) the plumber foreman, with residents whose names have been forgotten – sorry!

Govan Housing Association collection

The improved Taransay Street backcourt in 1976

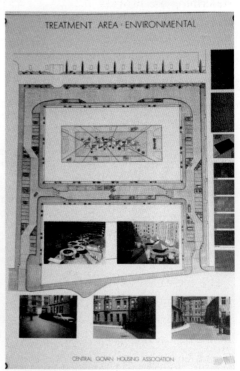

Proposals for Environmental works in the Treatment Area

7. Annie's loo starts a trend!

'A nice hot bath will fix just about anything.'

Anon

THE OPENING of Annie's loo was the turning point in the improvement programme. We had demonstrated that improvement work could be carried out on a voluntary basis, and that the multiple ownership nature of tenement areas could be retained. There were three immediate impacts.

First, having proved that a stack of bathrooms could be inserted, there was a product to sell. A real live bathroom! Annie's loo was marketed like a modern day show house for two weeks. And this was where the preplanning began to show its value. Leaflets describing the process, the specification and most importantly a fixed price were available, culminating in the quote from the satisfied customer – 'It's the best 190 quid's worth I have ever had, and I've been surprised with how little mess the workmen have made'. (Mrs Gibbons).

A member of the ASSIST team was there at all opening times, along with a member of the Fairfield Residents Association. If you wanted a similar bathroom all you needed to do was to call a meeting of everyone in your building (a 'close meeting') at which a member of ASSIST would attend, get your neighbours to agree that they wanted a bathroom too and your close would go onto the programme. There was to be no orderly pattern of improvement work – it would depend on the willingness of the occupants in which order the buildings were to be improved.

Sheila O'Halloran, the Secretary of the Residents Association, was seen taking her neighbours to view the show house, locking them in the bathroom and not letting them out until they had agreed to have one. The ASSIST team called it 'community participation'. Theo Crombie suggested that if the Corporation had used the same techniques, community activists would have called it 'harassment'!

Second, the Corporation was able take seriously the proposal for voluntary improvement. While the Corporation had declared the Taransay Street Treatment Area, it had not appointed anyone to co-ordinate it or to act as its agent. It had simply agreed not to use Compulsory Purchase Order powers in the meantime. The threat of CPO still hung over Taransay Street. Discussions with Theo and his team lead to a challenge – if the majority of owners had applied for a grant by the beginning of August 1972 the CPO threat would be removed and voluntary improvement accepted as the delivery mechanism.

Third, we were able to put ASSIST onto a more secure financial basis. When David Whitham came to visit the Gibbons' bathroom, the immerser was turned up high, the tap turned on and his hand forcibly put under it. 'Hot water, David – where's the money?' And he produced it. A grant of £20,000 – 50% of the running costs of ASSIST – was forthcoming from the Scottish Development Department, allowing ASSIST to seek funding from other sources.

The Wates Foundation matched the Government grant by making one of their very few awards outwith the South of England at the time.

While nothing formal was written down, this effectively meant that ASSIST was in a position to be the Corporation's agent – and indeed it was to take a central and coordinating role in the programme as it developed. We were able to attract additional staff. ASSIST had become a one of the earliest 'community architecture' practices – albeit part of the University. It was committed to working with the residents – it continued to provide the secretarial support to the Residents' Association and therefore to the principles of public participation. ASSIST provided a free technical service to owners in the Treatment Area. It continued to serve the Housing Association; but it also became the *de facto* agent of the Corporation. There was to develop a very close relationship with the Corporation – particularly with Theo Crombie and his team that included more key players for the future – Ronnie MacDonald and Denis Rogers.

During the spring and early summer of 1972, close meetings were held and followed up. By the beginning of August there had been a flurry of activity. Grant applications had been made on behalf of the majority of owners – including the landlords who owned outright six closes in Taransay Street. The Corporation's challenge had been met! It meant that a rolling programme could begin. Landlords keen to get out of the private rented sector and owner-occupiers who were unwilling or unable to improve began to sell to the housing association. Those who wanted to move were referred to the Housing Department, and in many cases their next door neighbours started the negotiation of buying their flat so that they could have a larger one. There was to be no set pattern – different floors in the same close could have different sizes of flats.

It was not all easy. There were some who wanted nothing done and they had to be persuaded to participate. In one case Tommy Barrie, the plumber foreman, was the person who persuaded a recluse to get involved because he discovered that the tenant (as he was) played the fiddle – as did Tommy! A Polish speaker (Jim Johnson's wife Krystyna) had to be asked to mediate with a lady who said that she only spoke Polish. One tenant chose the wrong time to be imprisoned; with the landlord's agreement and under police supervision his flat was improved while he was 'doing time'. In only one case was a bathroom not installed. An 80 year old lady tenant whose landlord sold the flat to the housing association thought that having an inside toilet was unhygienic. The Sanitary Inspector agreed that she could be left with sole use of the outside toilet, on the clear understanding that when she died the house would be improved! (Under the 1969 Act the house met the tolerable standard as she had sole use. And when she died the flat was improved!) And there was an unintended consequence in having the occupiers live in their homes during the period when their house was being improved – they became excellent Clerks of Works. Nothing escaped them!

With the programme now on stream, and finance being available, an office was rented. The Lord Provost of Glasgow, Sir William Gray, agreed to perform the opening ceremony in November 1972 for the ASSIST shop at 925 Govan Road. With its architectural red and black painted doors and windows, it was a 'community architecture' shop – one of the very first in the UK. Demand for the information service that Margo Weir had started grew dramatically – we became known as a source of advice and a more specialist approach had to be made.

One of the innovations that came about with having a proper

office was a weekly Corporation Planning Department surgery on progress within the CDA. This was proposed and sponsored by the New Govan Society – another benefit of its close relationship with the Corporation. Most of the enquiries concerned the demolition timetable; with people wanting to know about when their building was coming down and when they would be rehoused. This was also very much in keeping with the original spirit of the project – decentralised and local provision of public services. The office was also used for other services – a legal advice service was started (which would grow into the Govan Law Centre), and Councillors' surgeries (including Councillor Michael Martin – later to be Mr Speaker).

With the volume of enquiries growing, a full time community worker was appointed – Mike Thornley – partly to supervise the advice service, but also to help residents in the improvement programme with the financial, re-housing and other social issues. Mike was an architect and was soon to become much more involved on the architectural side of the business, with a 'proper' community worker – Marie Smith – being employed. Marie's appointment was not solely about the Treatment Area, but to give help and support to individuals and tenant groups within the CDA.

Marie's appointment coincided with the election of Margo MacDonald as SNP MP. Politics in Govan got a little tetchy, and inevitably some of the issues with which Marie was involved were advocacy on behalf of individuals with grievances against the Corporation. These led to some campaigning against the Corporation for which the same ASSIST was effectively acting as agent. This created some internal friction within ASSIST and between ASSIST and parts of the Corporation, because some of us were concerned to ensure that disputes did not impact negatively on the improvement programme. Perhaps some of us (me included) had become part of the system! The ghost of the Old Swan appeared!

We had started with the thought that working with the Corporation rather than in a confrontational mode would make life easier. But inevitably there are situations where real and perceived injustices require a more forthright approach to be taken. Sometimes change only comes about when issues are forced into the open through a more confrontational style – particularly if attempts to deal with the situation in a more reasoned way have failed. In the end, community politics means that while negotiation may be preferable, public confrontation may be required if the community feels that it is being ignored. At the heart of partnership working is the issue of power sharing, and like any other relationship, if one party feels that the other is not playing fair, then the partnership can crumble.

The success of the advice service was also in danger of crowding out the free architecture service – which was available not just for the Treatment Area but for Govan residents. However, demand for the technical service was also increasing. This caused some difficulties with the architectural profession, and Professor Tom Markus was hauled up in front of the Glasgow Institute of Architects to receive complaints about unfair competition from the University and its free architectural service. We were obviously doing something right!

As a University Project we were also of interest to students. Ian Macbeth came to do his practical training year. And Ronnie Murray continued a tradition established by Peter Robinson of looking at tenement issues for his thesis – this time looking at environmental improvements. He became known as the 'backcourt man', joined the team and organised the backcourt upgrading.

The programme was not without its difficulties. Contractors' performance was not always of the highest standard (and delays happened); clients could be awkward; payments by owners could be slow (or needed referring to the lawyers); the Central Govan Housing Association was always short of finance (raising its 25% share of building works and the purchase costs on unimproved properties was very difficult); and the ambition of ASSIST was not necessarily matched by either our resources or our administrative capabilities. However, 86% of all improvements carried out in Housing Treatment Areas in the city between 1970-74 were in Govan (Taransay Street) – and the Corporation had continued to declare HTAs during the period. The ownership pattern at the end of the programme in 1976 was an almost equal balance of owner-occupation, housing association and private rent.

There was an unexpected consequence of improving the Taransay Street Treatment Area. By putting in bathrooms the houses were no longer 'Below Tolerable Standard'. As such they were removed by the Sanitary Inspector from the sub-tolerable list and therefore no longer in danger of demolition. A short-life improvement project had become a rehabilitation or even a conservation project! This would have consequences – further and more intensive rehabilitation works would be required to ensure the long term sustainability of the tenement block.

Meanwhile, the voluntary improvement programme in Taransay Street and ASSIST was attracting interest from a number of other areas that were interested in what was being done in Govan – including Maryhill (where a young Councillor Vince Cable was to encourage a Queen's Cross Housing Association) and Govanhill (where Councillor the Rev. Geoff Shaw was also the Leader of the Corporation). By the close of 1973, Mike Thornley was working with the Govanhill community as an architect, developing effectively a second ASSIST and Govanhill Housing Association.

The time was ripe for an expansion of the programme. ASSIST was discussing with the Corporation how a number of ASSIST-type organisations could be created across the city. The Government in Scotland was reviewing progress with the 1969 Act while pressure was growing across the UK to give better support to housing associations. The reviews were to lead to new legislation while the Govan project attracted interest from a national housing organisation. Taransay Street was soon to become the prototype – with some changes – of a community based housing movement.

The ASSIST team in 1973 during the 3-day week outside the office at 925 Govan Road. They are (l to r): Marie Smith; Ronnie Murray; Sheila O'Halloran, Archie Provan, Rosemary Young; and Ian Macbeth

8. Housing Associations become key

'Each social formation, through each of its material
activities, exerts its influence upon the civic whole; and
each of its ideas and ideals wins also its place and power.'
Patrick Geddes

TWO ACTS of Parliament were passed in 1974. The Housing
(Scotland) Act 1974 upgraded the Tolerable Standard,
reinvented Housing Treatment Areas as Housing Action Areas
(HAAs), and improved the grant regime. It has been called 'the
Glasgow Act', since much of its provisions were designed to drive
the improvement of Glasgow tenements, following the experiences
of the city – partly in Govan. A small group led by Tom Duncan
from the Planning Exchange had fed reviews of the workings of the
1969 Act into the pre-drafting process and that group included
academics, local government officials (on an informal basis) and
the ASSIST team. (The Planning Exchange had been set up by and
was led by Professor Barry Cullingworth, the author of the 1965
report on Glasgow's housing stock.)

The Housing Act 1974 provided – for the whole of Great Britain
– a new regime for housing associations. The ability of housing
associations to deliver more homes was clearly being constrained
by the funding (or lack of funding) regime. Campaigns by Shelter
and the National Federation of Housing Societies led to a Housing
Bill being promoted first by the Heath Government in 1973. This
bill however fell with the Tory Government, but was picked up
almost word for word by the incoming Labour administration. So
it had full cross-party support – a position that was to be essential
in the years ahead. The new regime would provide funding in the
form of Housing Association Grant (HAG) and public sector loans
– providing the association was registered with the Housing
Corporation and subject to its regulation. The Housing Corporation
was a government agency that worked across Great Britain.

The new Chairman of the Housing Corporation was Lord
Goodman. He was appointed to transform the Housing Corporation

which had been created in 1964 to develop a niche market in co-ownership and cost rent societies. By the early 1970s the economic and housing policy conditions in which it had been created were completely different. Co-ownership and cost rent had appealed to a middle market; in the intervening years property speculation, gentrification, illegal evictions, private rented sector scandals and poor quality public sector housing along with the foundation of Shelter and other pressure groups made the Housing Corporation even more of a niche player.

Lord Goodman was considered by many to be the greatest negotiator of his age. He certainly had an unusual approach. The story is that when he became chairman he asked for two maps to be hung in his office – one of housing need and one of where housing associations were operating. Lord Goodman sent his private secretary, David Astor, to find out why Glasgow, with one of the highest levels of housing need in Great Britain, had so few housing associations. David Astor's approach to the city was also unconventional. He knew Geoff Shaw who was part of the Gorbals Group – a radical experiment in social gospel ministry within the Church of Scotland outside conventional parish structures. Geoff had been born into a wealthy Edinburgh family, but his ministry was with marginalised people in what was then still regarded as one of the worst slums in Europe. Geoff had decided that he had to get directly involved in politics and had been first a Labour councillor and by 1973 was the Leader of the administration. Once again, a church thread is woven into the story.

Geoff advised David Astor to visit ASSIST in Govan. His visit was followed by Lord Goodman, Dick Madge the Housing Corporation's Chief Executive and other senior executives. Discussions between the two Corporations (Glasgow Corporation and the Housing Corporation) then centred on how the Housing Corporation could help develop the Govan model across the city. Despite trying, there was no way in which either body could fund a series of community architecture shops; however one part of the Govan model was identified as being suitable to be replicated and developed – Central Govan Housing Association. The proposal, as it evolved, was that housing associations would become the City Corporation's agent in HAAs, co-ordinating improvement work, and funded by the Housing Corporation. This was to be quite a step for the City Corporation which was not noted for its enthusiasm for partnership working. As we have seen normally it liked to do things itself!

But a partnership deal was struck. The Housing Corporation would establish an office in Glasgow solely to deal with the Glasgow Rehabilitation Programme. So the Scottish Regional Office of the Housing Corporation, based in Edinburgh, came to visit ASSIST and to see not just Annie's loo, but Sheila's, Effie's and many others. The first meeting between the Edinburgh Office team (to which the Glasgow Office was to report) and the ASSIST team was not terribly comfortable – it could be described as a clash of cultures! We were housed in the windowless backroom of a Govan shop; their offices were in Edinburgh New Town. Our customers were local residents with the odd sprinkling and support of professionals; their customers were primarily professionally run housing societies. But there was a recognition that changes were required in the Housing Corporation and of the potential created by the new legislation.

Margo Weir sent me the advertisement for the head of the new Glasgow office, and insisted that I applied. Interviews were in London with both the Chief Executive and the Chairman, and not involving the Regional Manager in Edinburgh. This indicated the level of importance which the Housing Corporation was giving to the Glasgow Programme. I was appointed and moved from ASSIST on 1st April 1974. The independent streak in me insisted that the Glasgow office would be in Glasgow even although no office accommodation had been acquired and I would not work from a desk in Edinburgh. So we 'camped' in the Planning Exchange until offices were obtained!

The Plan was that the Housing Corporation would work with the National Building Agency (of which Lord Goodman was also chairman) as technical advisers. This lasted for a short period of time before Ronnie Murray joined the Housing Corporation team along with a young lawyer called Jim Hastie.

The partnership between the two Corporations (the Glasgow one was to disappear in 1975 under local government reorganisation and become Glasgow District Council) was overseen by a joint steering group of Councillors and Board members of the Housing Corporation (appointed by the Government of the day). The Housing Corporation established a Scottish Committee; its first Chairman was W.L. Taylor who had been a Glasgow Labour

Councillor in the 1950s and chair of the Planning Committee. So he knew his way around Glasgow Corporation both at member and official level. This reinforced the close working relationships at officer level – still led on the Glasgow side by Theo Crombie, supported by a team including Ronnie MacDonald and Denis Rogers. The Government's Scottish Housing Minister was Hugh Brown MP – a close personal friend of Bill Taylor.

There is no doubt that the success of the Glasgow Rehabilitation Programme and the growth of community based associations is partly due to the strong personal relationships of the various parties at the city level. As was the importance which the Housing Corporation's Chief Executive gave to the programme. Very quickly Dick Madge, and his Deputy John Baker, committed themselves to visiting Glasgow regularly. While formally those of us in the Glasgow Office reported through Edinburgh, the reality was that in the early days of the Glasgow office, we reported directly to the Chief Executive. In the partnership, the Housing Corporation played the junior partner. We were there to support Glasgow's Rehabilitation Programme with the city in the lead. This may be another key to the long term success – personal relationships on the one hand, but recognising the seniority and leadership of the city on the other. But the real success – just like in Govan – was the commitment and energy with which local residents responded to the opportunity to develop their own housing associations. They were backed by their local councillors – and an unusual 'cross bench' partnership that included John Ross for Labour and Iain Dyer for the Conservatives that was critical in ensuring the support of the Corporation.

If the first major difference with the Govan pilot was that housing associations would become the coordinator of the Housing Action Areas rather than a local architectural office fulfilling the role, the other major change was that the Glasgow Rehabilitation Programme was not about short-life improvement. None of the areas chosen for Housing Action Areas were designated for redevelopment – a lesson no doubt learnt from Taransay Street. A thirty year life was the target which meant a greater level of intervention, more extensive work and therefore higher capital investment. To suit this, the procurement system had also to change – the Master Document approach that Ian Sloan had devised was regrettably not considered suitable for the requirements of tendering and a more traditional contract approach had to be used.

Another of the features of the Govan pilot that was lost was that of the occupants remaining in the house while the work was underway. The amount of work that had to be done demanded temporary re-housing and gave rise to the word 'decanting' and its practice in relation to rehabilitation. Not everyone was decanted. Some took the opportunity to move elsewhere – usually within the neighbourhood. Although residents in a particular close were not always rehoused together, people remained within the community. Those that could were rehoused back into their own building.

The Housing Corporation's funding allowed for the associations to adopt higher standards which many lower income owner-occupiers could not afford, but the funding also enabled the same associations to buy out these owners, who could become tenants. Very quickly, and under Jim Hastie's legal administration, the Housing Corporation set up an Acquisition Service for housing associations. This central buying service worked in close harmony with the Glasgow Corporation's programme of Housing Action Area declaration – the programme being the result of the joint Scottish Development Department, Glasgow Corporation's House Improvement and Clearance Section and the city's Planning Department report. The impact of the thirty year life and the efficiency of the Acquisition Service meant that the ownership proportion of the new Housing Action Areas changed with housing associations owning between 90 and 100%. Compulsory Purchase Order powers were used to clarify titles or where the owner was unknown – not, as in the Old Swan and other Glasgow Corporation driven projects, to forcibly acquire whole buildings. CPO powers were used by the Housing Corporation (with the support of Glasgow) – indeed were the first use of CPO powers by the Housing Corporation.

One of the features of the Acquisition Service was that it could operate ahead of the creation of individual associations. A group of 'shadow' associations was created – each called the Glasgow Fair (name of area) Housing Association. Glasgow Fair is of course the annual trades two weeks holiday; there was a certain amount of humour in the title – certainly every one of them lasted somewhat longer than two weeks! The members of the Glasgow Fair associations were drawn from the two Corporations along with a representative of the Glasgow Property Owners and Factors Association. Jim Hastie acted as secretary.

Two community based associations preceded the partnership between the two Corporations – Central Govan and Govanhill. The latter had been quickly registered with the Registrar of Friendly Societies just in case the Housing Corporation wanted to create organisations other than community based associations! However, that fear was to be proven foundless. There were discussions about the nature of the associations – Dick Madge wondered whether a couple of city wide associations would be more effective. He was originally concerned whether the community based model would have sufficient skills to deal with the complexities of the new financial regime and the scrutiny required by registration.

At that time, the Housing Corporation was having difficulties with a number of existing associations involving governance, transparency and financial skills. Dick was persuaded, however, that voluntary improvement of HAAs in Scotland required local associations which would have membership open and representative of the area; while a Housing Corporation office dedicated to the development, support and funding of the Glasgow programme and particularly (but, we were advised, not exclusively) community based associations would mean that his Glasgow Office would be very close to the associations and should be able to see any warning signs that might mean that action should be taken to protect both the tenants and the public purse.

There were of course other associations operating in the city. These were mainly co-ownership associations having been recognised by the Housing Corporation since its inception in 1964. (Registration was first introduced by the 1974 Act.) They were run by estate agents, surveyors and similar property professionals. There were some meetings with them, but the expectations that they were given by those of us in the Glasgow Office, involving both improvement work and, in particular, the participation of the residents, seemed to make them less than enthusiastic. So nothing came of these. Christian Action (Glasgow) Housing Association was the exception – it continued, was supported by the Glasgow Office and worked in a number of areas partly outwith Housing Action Areas. It is now the West of Scotland Housing Association. Over time, a number of other associations which were formally operating outwith the Rehabilitation Programme were registered and supported.

The main role of the Housing Corporation's Glasgow Office

became that of working with the City Corporation to deliver housing associations which would act as that Corporation's agent in each of its Housing Action Areas.

The process for the establishment of the new associations was: Glasgow Corporation identified the areas to be improved; these would be areas of around 2,000-3,000 BTS houses; the plan was to declare a number of HAAs over a period of time, thus creating a rolling programme.

On declaration, a public meeting was called by Glasgow Corporation – normally chaired by a local councillor. City Council officials would explain the HAA process. Housing Corporation officials would then explain the role of a housing association and invite people to put themselves forward for an information and training programme over a few weeks looking at the responsibilities and the operation of a housing association. The Housing Corporation team was looking for volunteers, and we explained that the nature of the association was such that once registered (and seven was the minimum number needed for registration) membership would be open to all – tenants, owners and shopkeepers within the areas with BTS housing. At some meetings, we stressed that the existing landlords were not going to improve their houses, that the City Corporation did not wish to take over the houses, and that then only people that could improve their housing conditions were the residents themselves. The Housing Corporation would support them.

The training programme lasted about twelve weeks. It often started with a group of about twenty people; by the end some people would have dropped out, but still there were sufficient to make application for registration, first as an Industrial and Provident Society and then under the 1974 Act. The Housing Corporation agreed that these two processes, which normally had to be done one after the other, could be done concurrently. It took several months to have an association registered. The cost of the training programme (hire of halls etc, and the registration fees) were paid for out of a 'start-up' grant from Glasgow Corporation. This grant was designed to cover the early costs of developing an association until the acquisition and development allowances that were part of the HAG regime became available when flats began to be acquired.

While the training programme was underway, Jim Hastie as secretary of the appropriate Glasgow Fair HA started to notify the owners in the designated area of the option of selling and of using the Housing Corporation's streamlined procedures to acquire some properties. When the local association had been registered, any properties acquired by the Glasgow Fair association were transferred to the new association by merging the two bodies.

A further major help was that the Housing Corporation agreed that it should develop a programme of hiring and preparing potential staff for each of the associations. So a number of people were selected, employed by the Housing Corporation, and inducted into the way the associations would operate as agents of the City Corporation. They came from a variety of backgrounds – community development, Shelter and architects being among the group. They met with the committee of the new association, and if both parties felt that they could work with each other, then the association's first member of staff was appointed, and transferred to the association, which was given the 'start-up' grant. They were purposely not called 'Directors' because the association had to be given the opportunity of appointing to that position. They were called 'Development Officers' and had the twin role of developing the association as an organisation and of developing the improvement programme. The original thought was that the 'Development Officer' would be a temporary appointment and that he/she could help the development of a number of associations. The reality was that most worked so well with the new committee that they became the Director! They came from a variety of backgrounds – social work, community work, a trade union organiser, and young academics.

Within the first two years new associations had been established in Linthouse, Tollcross, Elderpark, Partick, Queen's Cross, Shettleston, Reidvale, and Springburn – mainly in the old burghs surrounding the city's central business district.

This approach to the development of the Glasgow Rehabilitation Programme also impacted on the consultants that were appointed by each association to undertake the improvement work. Working in the evening with local committees did not appeal to many traditional firms of architects. ASSIST continued to support a number; while a group of new younger practices emerged with an

Howat Street, looking up to Taransay Street and the great wall (now decorated with murals) in 2012

understanding of traditional building techniques and an ability to work with local communities – and not just in HAAs.

Most importantly, there emerged a whole new group of residents who ran the community based housing associations. They developed a network of skilled, articulate volunteers who would demand higher quality and, although they might not have used the language, would be at the forefront of 'Urban Development' and 'Conservation', appreciating the value and sustainability that good rehabilitation and conservation brings to communities, restoring pride in their neighbourhood, as well as using the skills learnt in a wide range of community activities and community engagement. The story of people like John Butterley in Reidvale, Helen MacGregor in Tollcross, Eddie McEachan in Elderpark, Flora Glen in Govan and Betty Stevenson in Govanhill and many more could fill many more pages, but this book is about beginnings, and a line must be drawn somewhere.

However, I want to conclude with some reflections about the impact of all this forty years on.

Forty years on

. . . and community based associations are part of a major housing sector in Scotland providing social rented housing and much more.

During the 1970s and 1980s housing associations became a major force for the improvement of inner city tenements – not just in Glasgow. In the east of Scotland, there had been improvements undertaken by private landlords in single ownership tenement blocks. For example in Dundee, action by house factor Russell Milne led to the establishment of Tay Valley Housing Association. In Edinburgh the City Corporation had developed an approach that saw the City use its 'by law' powers and other statutory powers to coordinate work in Housing Association Areas. With the support of the Housing Corporation, the city oversaw the creation of a group of associations similar to the community based ones in Glasgow in places like Fountainbridge and Leith.

The concept of local community control in housing and its involvement in the rehabilitation of tenements was to become a distinctive characteristic of much of the Scottish housing association movement. It was even to produce a legislative definition. While the Housing Corporation's Glasgow office had been set up to support the Glasgow Rehabilitation programme, requests from other local authorities within Strathclyde led to the development of community based associations in Motherwell, Paisley, Cunninghame and Argyll.

The growth of housing associations in the 70s and 80s was fuelled by large amounts of public finance channelled through the Housing Corporation. The original proposals for Housing Association Grant was made by the Heath Government in 1973, implemented by the Wilson Government in 1974 and continued by the Conservative Government under Margaret Thatcher. This cross-party support was particularly effective in Scotland, where the support of consecutive Secretaries of State – especially George Younger and Malcolm Rifkind – was important. The Conservative Government looked upon associations as a desirable alternative to local authorities, while the local authorities (mainly Labour-led) considered that associations were undertaking work which they (local authorities) felt that they were either unable to do (rehabilitation of privately owned tenements) or which they regarded as specialised housing provision.

It was not all plain sailing! There were small and large battles to be won, and they were fought with passion and sometimes with unorthodox methods. Control of the Housing Corporation programme was switched from the number of units approved to the commitment of annual expenditure. Around that time expenditure seemed to be overheating in the state-sponsored housing agency Scottish Special Housing Association (SSHA) with a small, centrally controlled programme. But then senior civil servants became very nervous about the Housing Corporation's ability to manage within the limits: if SSHA could get it wrong, how much more damage could these young inexperienced people do? And they brought the programme to a shuddering halt in the nightmare called 'the moratorium'. A group of Glasgow committee members cycled to London – pre-devolution – to highlight their case for resources when public expenditure cutbacks threatened to disrupt the programme. And there were battles over the need for rising standards such as central heating. One of the interesting ways in which changes occurred was when the Housing Corporation could take up a 'behind-the-scenes' lobbying role in support of the associations with which senior staff agreed even although it had to publicly support the Government's position. Such was the closeness of the relationships.

Nor is the programme complete some forty years later. There still remain some small pockets of 'Below Tolerable Standard' (BTS) housing which are waiting to be improved, while resources have never completely matched either the scale of the challenge or the aspirations of communities. Housing Association Grant (HAG) may be the longest lasting housing subsidy in the history of financial support for the housing sector, but as the scale of the sector increased, and public funds became tighter, the rules changed. First, in the mid 1980s loans from the public sector amounting to less than 10% of the total costs were replaced by private borrowing finance. This was designed to make public funding go further and then in the 1990s the HAG levels were progressively reduced with a corresponding increase in the contribution of private money. And so on over the years, the target for subsidy was reduced and more money came to be borrowed from banks and building societies.

By 1986, however, moves were made to adapt the community based model to some of the more 'hard to live in' areas of local authority housing. The first two of these were in ;tlemilk and

Easterhouse in Glasgow. The houses were acquired by agreement from the Council. Because the properties were all in single ownership, a fully mutual co-operative version of community based approach was developed, with the tenants being the shareholders, and the shareholders being the tenants. This was followed by the transfer of local authority houses in Perth to Fairfield Housing Cooperative. For these tenants, stock transfer was accompanied by a publicly-funded regeneration programme, involving the houses and the environment coupled with social and economic change. This in turn influenced the foundation of a major national regeneration programme covering four large scale local authority estates – one each in Glasgow, Edinburgh, Dundee and Paisley under the banner 'New Life for Urban Scotland' – and involving associations working alongside the whole range of national government agencies.

1989 brought the merger of the Housing Corporation in Scotland and the SSHA to create Scottish Homes. By then, housing associations had become the normal method of providing new social housing, and local authorities had virtually stopped building new housing. The Right to Buy (RTB), introduced in 1980, was highly popular, with owner-occupation growing rapidly in Scotland. RTB had a major impact on the size of the local authority stock, with Councils being unable to replace lost stock through new build. Meanwhile, housing associations were encouraged to develop the community based and cooperative model through transfers from the public sector. These were applied to Scottish Homes stock and to more council owned housing. The first transfers were in the Borders and thereafter a number other councils, for example Dumfries and Galloway, took advantage of transfer. The largest of all was the transfer of Glasgow City stock to Glasgow Housing Association.

Scottish Homes also developed the work that the Housing Corporation had started in sponsoring housing associations in rural Scotland. Many of them exhibit the same community based approach that had begun in Govan – locally based (albeit on a wider geographical area), of medium size, with an open membership policy, and working closely with other community organisations. Like many of their urban counterparts they have become community enterprises – taking on roles that are housing based but provide a wider range of services like Care and Repair which helps older owner-occupiers maintain their homes and provides them with the support to stay longer in their own community. In the Highlands and Islands these local associations follow a tradition of community co-operatives established with the support of the Highlands and Islands Development Board (now Highlands and Islands Enterprise) in a programme that was similar to that of the Housing Corporation, but developing local business. Community land ownership has grown significantly following the Land Reform (Scotland) Act 2003, and housing associations have made their contribution to the 'Community Right to Buy' programme in places like Gigha.

In less than 40 years, the tenure of the housing stock in Scotland has been transformed by these developments. There were three key strands in the increasing role for associations: acquisition from the private sector for rehabilitation; new building for general and special needs; acquisition (transfer) from the public sector for regeneration and renewal.

While housing associations have made a significant contribution to the change, the greatest impact has been through the right-to-buy. The table below shows the changes. In 1971 local authorities dominated the picture; housing associations were so small that they were included in the private rented sector. By 2011, owner-occupation had risen to over 61%, and the public sector had declined to 13%.The private rented sector has made a comeback – though not to 1971 levels. Housing association ownership has grown dramatically because of transfers from the public sector.

Tenure in Scotland in 40 years	1971	1981	1991	2001	2011
Owner-occupiers	31%	36%	52%	60%	61%
Private renting	17%	10%	6%	7%	12%
Public sector (incl New Town and SSHA	52%	52%	40%	24%	13%
Housing Associations	in private rented	2%	3%	6%	11%
Vacant	n/a	n/a	n/a	3%	4%

(All figures rounded. Sources: Wilcox, S (ed.) (annual) UK Housing Review Chartered Institute of Housing, Coventry and Building Societies Association, London; Scottish Housing Statistics)

In these forty years, associations have achieved much. Alan Murie, in his history of the Housing Corporation, describes the Scottish housing associations as having a 'distinctive approach' through their community base in comparison to those in the rest of Great Britain.

This 'distinctive approach' remains today. Although the approach may be seen most clearly in the west of Scotland, the promotion and close working relationship between the Housing Corporation and associations was not simply a feature of the west of Scotland. The pattern of community involvement in housing associations operates right across the country. The majority of associations operate in a specific geographical area, most are small to medium size (around 1500 – 2000 units) with membership open to people in the local community. They sit alongside local economic and social enterprises. But the 'distinctive approach' has influenced the whole sector – and not just those who are based in one geographical area.

Part of the growth has seen associations do more than simply provide houses for rent. They provide help to people who aspire to home ownership through shared ownership and partnerships with developers. They provide management services to owner-occupiers – very important in tenements, both the improved Victorian tenements like those which include the Govan flats, but also modern walk-up flats.

They are social and regeneration agencies, providing support not only to their own tenants but to the local community. The activities might range from wind turbines which generate alternative sources of income; to community cafes to help older people combat social isolation. This wider activity was for a time part funded by the Government agency that followed Scottish Homes – Communities Scotland. The funding arrangements were through a scheme called 'Wider Role Fund' that saw associations tackle a range of projects largely in areas of socio-economic need. It was particularly useful for unlocking other sources of public grant funding for regeneration activity.

The contribution which associations make to neighbourhood regeneration has therefore become another 'distinctive' feature. Many are the linchpin of a community based approach. They provide employment and training opportunities, social care, and support to immigrants and asylum seekers. Some offer a secure cashpoint, or a community centre with IT facilities for local residents. They do so either directly, or through subsidiary organisations that have been created as a result of the association's understanding the needs of its neighbourhood and the experience built up through running a housing association. Some run social enterprises including furniture recycling, or cleaning services, some seek to assist with advice and financial inclusion. They are now social entrepreneurs and run successful and complex businesses.

Kim McKee, an academic from the University of St Andrews, sets out what has been accomplished by the community based approach in particular:

> During the last 35 years the community housing movement has delivered many benefits for Scotland's communities. As well as bringing physical investment through renewal and rehabilitation programmes, they have also delivered community empowerment and local accountability. They encourage active citizenship through tenant involvement and management in the houses, with committee members having control and influence over financial and management resources. Neighbourhood offices and committees also ensure accountability to tenants locally, as well as offering a more responsive and personalised service. . .

Yet community housing provides more than just bricks and mortar. The sector has played a key role in local regeneration initiatives and wider action, for example supporting small community enterprises, community education and training, workspaces, affordable childcare, community arts and so forth. These activities have been vital in transforming the future of some of Scotland's most deprived communities and improving the opportunities open to local residents. It is these positive attributes of the sector that have earned it the mantra 'small is beautiful'.

So what is it that has made this success? My own view is that the serendipity coming from a combination of events, people and resources made possible the move from Govan pilot to city wide programme and beyond. This combination also made the growth from inner city tenement to a wider community programme in local estates. Developments outwith urban areas also required the same approach to local and national partnership working, the supportive network, and above all local leadership. The combination can be seen as:

The need for a new / different model

The large scale redevelopment plans typified by the Comprehensive Development Areas were proving to be too costly, and too slow to provide a decent home for everyone. They were also becoming unpopular. The unpopularity was partly about the sterility of the new and the absence of facilities. And that was translated into a lack of 'community'. (We now know that some of the estates which were originally seen as popular became unpopular, but are now – with hard work and time – stronger communities in their own right). So despite the disadvantages of high density tenement living, rehabilitation became an option that had to be investigated.

The scale provided by local housing associations

The local authority was more used to a butcher's cleaver approach in rehabilitation, when what was required was more of a surgical knife. Whoever carried out the rehabilitation, needed to be closer to the people affected for them to benefit. A voluntary association was part of the solution and once started, other benefits of this approach became plain. In particular, associations could hold communities together and this became even clearer when the associations undertook other social and economic activities in their neighbourhood. Unlike many rehabilitation programmes elsewhere in the UK, the community based approach appears to have supported community regeneration and avoided major gentrification.

Political support

The cross-party support that associations enjoyed (and still enjoy) saved associations from becoming a political football – both at national and local level. It meant a continuity of political support through the development of policy; changes that were made would have been made by any political party. At a city or council level, a local councillor represented the Council on the management committee of most community based associations, giving the associations a powerful lobby in the City Chambers.

The level of funding available

Although the Housing Association Grant (HAG) funding rules changed the level of commitment remained high. Other forms of funding were also important – particularly the 'start up' funding from Glasgow Corporation (and subsequently from other local authorities). The HAG system also ensured that associations were creating maintenance sinking funds which have enabled better long-term maintenance and asset management than that available to local authorities. While they enjoyed high levels of public finance, the governance structures meant that they could not be regarded as 'public bodies'. Nor could they be regarded as 'private sector bodies', but as a not-for-profit voluntary sector combining some of the best features of both – including financial rigour and public accountability.

The relationship between the local and specialist Corporations

The strategy would not have worked without a good working relationship between them. This applied at both member and officer level. There was great openness and trust between key officers in both Glasgow Corporation and the Housing Corporation, particularly its Glasgow Office. At one point a London based member of the Housing Corporation staff accused the Glasgow Office of being Glasgow Corporation's housing association department, which we in the Housing Corporation took as a compliment! But scale may have been a benefit. The Housing Corporation was small and therefore seen as the junior partner. Its successors had a more diverse role; they were also seen as having more politically driven agenda. However, personal relationships often overcame any concerns about other agendas.

The way the Housing Corporation worked with the associations

This applied to both the promotion phase and the continuing relationship. A more 'hands on' approach than was usual for the Housing Corporation meant that the Housing Corporation had a greater impact on how the associations developed. But it also meant that the Housing Corporation had early warning of problems and was able to move quickly and intervene where necessary. Thus the community based associations had fewer regulatory problems than many others in their early development phase. The relationship between Housing Corporation and the community based associations had the full backing of the Corporation's Chief Executive. The level of internal delegation was equally important – and it worked through the organisation with funding approvals delegated to staff working with the client associations. There was a team spirit involving both Corporations and the associations; a feeling that there was a joint programme even when there were differences (and there were).

The right kind of people working for associations

In the early days the programme attracted a particular kind of person to be staff members of both the Housing Corporation and associations. The primary requirements were their experience and/or willingness to work with local communities, and to bring some relevant skill. They came from a variety of backgrounds – some had been involved in campaigning, in trade union activities, in legal advice, in community architecture. All had a pioneering spirit and 'let's try it' approach and therefore set the tone for further staff recruitment.

The support network

The Scottish Federation of Housing Associations (SFHA) has had a national presence from 1975 taking over the Scottish arm of the National Federation. It has been the lead 'trade organisation' for associations with Government at Ministerial and official level. Other organisations have helped to support and develop the movement. Legal and technical consultants provide professional capacity; with SHARE as a Glasgow based training agency; EVH (Employers in Voluntary Housing) as the name suggests providing voluntary housing bodies with personnel and human resource management services. EVH began in Glasgow by giving support to voluntary committee members in salary and conditions negotiations with trade unions representing association staff and now operates across Scotland. Local forums in Glasgow, Edinburgh, Tayside, Grampian and rural Scotland provided a place for associations to share their concerns and plan campaigns. There was also a certain amount of peer support.

Leadership

This was by far the most important reason why it worked. In Glasgow, Theo Crombie had a 'fatherly' role – he was trusted by everyone and provided a stable, calming presence when the rest of us were getting too emotional. Every project needs that kind of leader. And local community leaders seized the opportunity to improve their housing and their neighbourhood. Had these residents not responded in the way they did, then none of the rest of the reasons for success would have mattered. Most of those who took up the challenge at the beginning had already been involved within their neighbourhood, but by joining and leading an association they developed city wide and national roles. For many their commitment was long term – without really realising what they were getting into they gave years of service to the improvement of their community. There is a study waiting to be done about those local leaders and the lessons that could be drawn for future regeneration programmes.

So does the future look rosy for housing associations? Not necessarily. There are significant challenges ahead.

Funding

Just like everyone else, associations are affected by the current economic climate. Public investment has been severely cut back and future development programmes reduced with increasing reliance on alternative sources of finance and new markets which present greater risks as well as opportunities. The development of housing associations as providers of housing for lower income groups has seen them move into markets which are quite different from social rent. They are now encouraged or required to deliver shared ownership programmes and other ways of encouraging people into home ownership. Many associations have been success-ful in this, which helps to create mixed tenure communities. However, the current grant levels impact on the ability of the associations as they are organised to grow to meet the continuing demand for lower cost rented housing – their original purpose. But the changes have meant more than 'less public finance'. In the growth days of the 1970s and 80s, effectively financial risks were carried by the public purse in return for Housing Corporation supervision and close involvement. Now the risks are carried by the associations who are more exposed to the financial markets, some significantly.

The future of nineteenth century tenements

While the last forty years have seen the tenements improved with better facilities and have been better managed where associations have become the factor, some have already passed their thirty year life expectancy. A further round of upgrading may be required. Without some major remodelling the tenements themselves may not meet rising aspirations. The smaller two or three roomed flats may not be what a young couple with a family expects. So new thinking will be required to ensure that the tenement continues to be in demand.

Many housing association tenants are in fuel poverty. Developmental work into improving the energy efficiency of tenements has been undertaken over the last few years. New partnerships are being formed – including with Historic Scotland, which has been undertaking research into energy efficiency and how tenements can be brought up to modern energy standards at an economic cost. And all of this is complicated by the re-fragmentation of ownership following right-to-buy. However, there are many reasons for continuing to invest in the tenements. The important contribution they can make to the national Climate Change Action Plan is only one element; tenements continue to be the core of the inner urban areas (where much of the new building is a 'tenemental' form) and they can therefore help to underpin the social, economic and environmental sustainability of these neighbourhoods, provided they are maintained.

Welfare Reform

Add to this mix the welfare reform agenda which looms over everything like Banquo's ghost. Three factors are likely to have a major impact on associations' rental income and operation in future: the reduction in eligibility of tenants for support with rent; the imminent replacement of Housing Benefit with the Universal Credit; and single / combined monthly payments.

Rationalisation and mergers

There is a question about the size of smaller associations. The average Scottish housing association has around 1500 houses and operates in a small geographical area in cities or a distinct rural community. In these austere times there are significant pressures on reducing overhead costs, and in many cases the response to these is seen through alliances and mergers. The word 'rationalisation' is used assuming that economies of scale deliver greater efficiency. Some sections of the housing association sector have already seen mergers. In creating bigger associations, there is a risk that committees/boards become detached from their original area of operation. And, according to governance experts, larger associations need a different kind of voluntary committee / board member – with more professional skills and so better equipped to manage larger organisations and the financial challenges that lie ahead. But those challenges affect everyone at every scale.

What has happened, of course, is that associations are no longer simply a niche player in locally based tenement rehabilitation or specialised housing provision. Housing associations are now part of the institutional structure of Scotland. Termed 'Registered Social Landlords' (RSLs); they are subject to the supervision of the new and independent Scottish Housing Regulator, established in April 2012 under the Housing (Scotland) Act 2010. The sector now has a wide range of organisations with differing needs and approaches and operating on different scales. Some are now large organisations operating across local authority boundaries and as part of UK conglomerates. Glasgow Housing Association as one of the largest social landlords in Europe has 37,000 properties (after transferring 19,000 houses and flats to local associations). The scale of even the most modest association, the level of public accountability, and the complexities of financing mean that all associations are managed by professional and specialist staff. A far cry from the days when Jim Stephen of Central Govan Housing Association rattled the can looking for funds, and Jim Hewitson factored the flats!

These changes may be inevitable. History gives examples of small community based movements growing into large national and international organisations. Savings banks and building societies are only two of them. And new kinds of local and community organisations emerge over time. Development Trusts, set up to acquire, develop and protect assets and services for their local community, have some of the same characteristics of the earlier housing associations – a voluntary response to a perceived local need making use of national policies. Several housing associations have either worked closely with a local Development Trust or set one up as a subsidiary.

A key issue is the empowerment which comes from involvement of the volunteer – whether at local or national level. Housing associations have undertaken social and economic programmes that have created communities of confidence. They have provided the basis for many people in so called 'deprived neighbourhoods' with the opportunity to manage change in their own communities, and to grow in self confidence. This fits very strongly with successive Government's regeneration policies. Since devolution in 1999, Scottish Governments have talked about community empowerment as a key component of transforming areas of social inclusion.

As an example – and one that sits with the architectural thread of this story – is the important way in which housing associations helped to empower communities by commissioning and working with design teams. A number of today's leading Scottish architects honed their skills in conjunction with local people in housing associations. It was a two way learning process. Working with architects, with surveyors and with contractors is a crucially empowering process for individuals in communities who are then justifiably proud of having been involved in the process – 'I was involved in that development; I have made a contribution to my community'. Charles McKean, then Secretary of the Royal Incorporation of Architects in Scotland even commissioned a drawing entitled 'the Medicis of Maryhill', featuring the Maryhill Housing Association committee, to demonstrate the importance of the voluntary committee as a good and educated client and a leader in urban regeneration.

Measuring the value of voluntary effort not only to the neighbourhood but to the nation and its wider benefits may be difficult, but its importance should not be lost sight of when the future of housing associations is being considered by regulators or funders. There is a danger that the most sought after volunteers are only those with business acumen and governance know-how as if the expertise that comes from living in the neighbourhood is at best of secondary importance. Local volunteers, with local knowledge, bring to the management committee an understanding of the issues facing the association in relation to its tenants, other stakeholders and the wider community. Even the word 'volunteer' itself is potentially disappearing, since recent legislation allows for committee members to be paid; it also allows staff to become members of the governing board. The irony of the latter is that this separation within the governance model of volunteers and benefits (particularly payments) was the very issue which Dick Madge was fighting about when the question of the kind of housing association for Glasgow was being discussed in 1974!

In conclusion. . .

Forty years after Annie's loo was first installed, housing associations have new challenges to face. The benign environment in which they began, and for many years enjoyed, is gone. The days of high public expenditure on housing are over – at least for a while, and probably for ever. Many associations managed significant change during these last forty years; once again those that manage change over the next period are likely to be the survivors. With new development projects thin on the ground, one of the major challenges will be to uphold a high standard of maintenance and housing management. Development can be a bit of a drug; maintenance and management is less compelling, and perversely, particularly if properties are well managed. Getting and keeping volunteers interested in running a smooth organisation without the excitement of new developments will be a further challenge. As will the need to balance financial management and governance with action to provide more homes and solve some of the wider but interrelated problems of the local neighbourhood, such as rising unemployment and wasted youth.

The future will require innovation and taking risks. But associations have done this before. Their track record in terms of regulation has been good. Hopefully, this will mean that the new regulatory system will not overly restrict or constrain their opportunities and activities, but will support them to take on future challenges. In developing to this point in time associations have continued to enjoy the cross party political support upon which they were founded, have established and nurtured good relationships and trust with a wide range of partners, both at institutional and personal level, and have shown leadership in times of difficulties. And they have shown themselves to be 'sustainable' in all of its manifestations – social cohesion, economic stability and environmental awareness. These must stand them in good stead for the future.

As part of the housing association sector those community based associations which began in Govan have offered a way in which the consumer, if he or she wishes, can be at the heart of the process, can get involved, and exercise some control. In doing so, they have made a significant contribution to the housing and regeneration story of Scotland. It is a contribution that requires wider recognition. The nation should celebrate the success of these associations, should recognise the unique contribution that they have made and ensure that they can continue to make a contribution to some of the most disadvantaged communities and families in Scotland – both rural and urban.

And finally. . .

This story has been about beginnings, what some people would call 'roots'. As housing associations face changes, it is hoped that these roots and the courage of the volunteers who said 'yes' over the last forty years will not be forgotten. And could policy makers remember that leadership comes in many guises, and that serendipity is often critical to the success of a policy?

The twenty first century tenement – built by Maryhill Housing Association in 1984-88, following an international architectural competition. Final design was by Ken McCrae, with McGurn, Logan, Duncan and Opfer

Govan Road with new housing by Govan Housing Association in 2005

Fairfield Housing Cooperative in Perth purchased and transformed a local authority housing estate. Shortlisted for a 'World Habitat Award' in 2003

Postscript

WHERE are they now? What has happened to some of the key players in this story?

Taransay Street

. . . is still there. It's been improved several times. Not only have the houses been improved, but environmental works have also been carried out to the streets. And it is still known as 'the Treatment Area'.

People

Of the key people in the story, there is quite a list of people who are no longer with us. John Gibbons died in 1995 and Annie moved to a new Central Govan Housing Association flat on Govan Road where she lived until she passed away in 2006. (A number of people in Govan knew her as Nancy; however all the papers from the early days call her Annie). Willie McShane, Barbara McDougall and Margo Weir have all gone. However, the O'Halloran's still live in Elder Street. Theo Crombie became Depute Town Clerk and has now retired to Inverness. Ronnie MacDonald and Jim Hastie have retired. Ronnie Murray and Mike Thornley set up their own architectural practices. And they too have now retired. Jim Johnson eventually left ASSIST and became the Director of the Edinburgh Old Town Renewal Trust. He is also the only survivor from the original Central Govan Committee and attended the Association's 40th birthday party in February 2011 along with Denis Rogers who was the last of Glasgow's House Improvement and Clearance Section to still be working for Glasgow City Council. As for me, I never did finish the degree!

Organisations

The Fairfield Residents Association gave way to Central Govan Housing Association as the main place for a community housing voice.

The New Govan Society was wound up in 1979 because David Orr and the committee decided that it was no longer needed – there were now a variety of bodies in Govan, all of which the New Govan Society had helped to bring into existence. So rather than find a new use (or like many organisations just keep going until it has a slow death), it was wound up! Throughout its life, David Orr led it, set the tone and kept on tying it back to the Pearce Institute. and to the church. It was almost as if he had found a way for a middle class minister to work out his faith in a new way – alongside the way that people like Geoff Shaw did, who took an active part in politics. Political commitment in a pluralistic society meant more than just the traditional political processes. Faith commitment in a secular society meant a lot more than the traditional church processes

The Pearce Institute survived a period of closure, but is now being re-born, partly to serve the local community, partly as a conference centre. Govan Housing Association has played a major role in its rebirth both through being a channel of Government funding through the Wider Action Fund, and by providing much needed management skills through membership of the PI committee and providing employment services.

Govan Old Parish Church is now part of a wider parish – Govan and Linthouse. The great building with its collection of stones is used for church services Monday to Friday and is in the process of becoming a major tourist attraction. With the new Riverside Museum on the north bank of the river, a part time ferry service now links Govan and Partick once more; the most enjoyable way to the new Museum is via the underground and the ferry.

But of course the church involvement in this story was never about church services or of soliciting for members. The role of the church and other faith groups (or more precisely members of faith groups, because the formal structures normally do not get involved but allow or facilitate members to be involved) was in taking action to help those who were in housing need (e.g. the establishment of a housing association) or in helping to ensure that the community had a voice in its own future. And that involvement still continues. Many voluntary committee members and many professional staff are involved in housing associations and other regeneration activities as a response to their faith belief – their faith calls them to use their time and skills to tackle issues of social injustice.

ASSIST

The original ASSIST badge – a repaint by Jim Johnson of the old tyre sign outside 925 Govan Road

ASSIST stayed in Govan until 1976 when the original work on the Taransay Street Housing Action Area was finished. By then it was working with community based housing associations across the city and had established offices in Govanhill, Linthouse and Reidvale. Its association with Govan was to continue. ASSIST continued to be commissioned by Central Govan Housing Association, but also for other clients becoming a more general architectural practice. Its clients tended to be innovative in themselves – for example the Glasgow Building Preservation Trust (which it helped to establish), and Govan Workspace Ltd. It was still 'a research project of the University of Strathclyde'; however the relationship with the university became increasingly difficult, and in 1984 it severed formal connections and was reformed as ASSIST Architects Ltd – the first architectural cooperative in Scotland. At the same time Jim Johnson left the University to be part of the cooperative. ASSIST continued pioneering work with housing associations including the new cooperatives in the peripheral housing estates and work on brownfield land. Early in its work it grew to encompass common repairs and environmental improvements. As in other projects, the participation of owners and tenants were paramount. Realising that maintenance was a critical issue for many tenement owners, John Gilbert and Ann Flint from ASSIST produced the definitive and practical guidebook to living in a tenement – *The Tenement Handbook*.

In the mid 1990s, ASSIST opened its Edinburgh office and developed a client base in the East of Scotland – including housing associations. It continues to be known for its community based approach, with strong emphasis on innovation, partnering procurement processes, wider action, inclusive and barrier free design, energy and sustainability.

ASSIST has had a wider impact. When the Housing Corporation/ Glasgow Corporation partnership was established, the scale of the programme required a considerable number of design skills. To begin with the National Building Agency was expected to play a major part, but more was required. Individual housing associations wanted to appoint their own architects. Many traditional practices were put off by having to work with the community as clients which involved evening working and in old tenements. As a result a whole breed of young architectural practices emerged from the community based approach – many of the teams having started with ASSIST. Now forty years on, many of them are respected members of the profession – John Gilbert, Ronnie Murray, MAST, and others – and are ready to or already have retired! A second generation of practices with experience of working with community clients now exists – many of whom are award winning names in Scotland – e.g. Elder and Canon; Page and Park; Gaia. Socially aware architects continue; and the community based housing associations continue to commission them as well as having helped to bring new thinking to the relationships between architect and client.

Central Govan Housing Association is flourishing, and is also typical of how the early community based associations have developed. It dropped the 'Central' to reflect that it now operates across a wider area than the tightly defined Taransay Street Housing Treatment Area, and now is simply called Govan Housing Association (GHA).

Over its life, GHA has changed and developed. It changed its rules to enable it to be a charitable housing association. For some time, it had a flourishing in-house architectural team, including Jim Johnson's wife Krystyna.

While tenements were its original housing type, it now (October 2012) has 1393 houses to rent. It offers a range of property from refurbished traditional sandstone tenements to newly built townhouses. Renting remains its core business. However, it provides management services to 477 owner-occupiers and 80 commercial premises. GHA has promoted low cost owner occupation in Govan with the development of shared ownership properties and has worked with developers to provide housing for outright sale. It has explored new opportunities to create affordable housing in Govan – the latest developments include an improvement for sale project and investigating 'homestake' options. The Association has also developed accommodation for particular client groups. This has included accessible accommodation for wheelchair users, sheltered and very sheltered housing for older people. The Association also provides a property management service for domestic and commercial owners

Govan Housing Association's latest development (completed 2012) and a good example of how community based associations continue to be at the forefront of both design and development. A mixed tenure project (for sale and for rent) jointly developed with Crudens, and designed by Adrian Shepherd of DO Architecture, a young award winning Glasgow based architectural practice

However, the association does more than provide houses. It works in partnership with a wide range of other organisations. For example, GHA has, in partnership with specialist agencies, provided 24 hour supported accommodation for people with learning difficulties and a project for people with mental health problems. Under the Government's Wider Role Fund, the association appointed an Ethnic Minority Outreach Worker; worked closely with Govan Initiative on helping to provide community meeting places; and remains involved with the redevelopment of the Pearce Institute. In the 1980s it helped sponsor the Govan Festival.

The Committee of ten is still made up of local residents elected by the membership which by October 2012 stood at 215. Amongst its past chairpersons is Michael O'Halloran – the husband of Sheila, the original Secretary of the Fairfield Residents Association.

GHA has 35 staff, including 3 modern apprentices. Its offices are in the centre of Govan – in the old Labour Exchange in McKechnie Street – and surrounded by houses it owns and manages. It remains firmly rooted in its community.

Its latest housing development typifies the way in which housing associations are changing to confront the new realities. A joint development with Cruden Estates has created 102 new flats (or apartments as we have come to call them) at Golspie Street. As these projects must now be, it involves a mixture of tenures – flats for rent, for shared ownership and for sale. However, it is more than just another block of flats. Its location is at the edge of the Govan Cross Conservation Area. A young and upcoming firm of architects – DO Architecture – was employed and the buildings make a statement. The long façade on Golspie Street is broken up into smaller more manageable blocks and there are large 'bays' with strong colours that make reference to the colours in local 'wally tile' closes. The backcourt is used for parking and communal activities and is entered by a 'pend'. The development swaggers a little; it could only have been produced by a client whose Management Committee members had a growing confidence in themselves and in their area. It shows ambition for Govan; a willingness to take risk; an entrepreneurial spirit which will be needed in the future. But it also remembers its roots and the people for whom it exists.

A symbol of Govan regeneration – the restored but waterless drinking fountain at Govan Cross. Compare this with the photo on page 54

Govan is at long last beginning to re-awaken, but it will take a long time. We know that regeneration is not simply about physical change, but even that takes longer that planned. As for the people – many have moved away. 'Ah-cum-fae-Govan' is still a proud boast, but few who have left have been enticed back. Govan Housing Association has been critical in helping Govan as a community through some very difficult times. The CDA programme which was to last fifteen years from 1968 is but an incomplete memory. Parts of the CDA were carried out; significant demolition and new building took place. A large number of tenements have been improved and new housing for sale and rent built. Some of the buildings planned by the CDA have already outlived their usefulness – like one new school which has been built, demolished and replaced by new housing within the forty years. Some of the multi storey developments are coming down.

Fairfield's shipyard has changed hands several times since the Upper Clyde Shipbuilders days, but it has survived and is now BVT Surface Fleet Govan, highly modernised and re-equipped, and having a major role in the new aircraft carriers. Most of the rest of the industrial past has gone, replaced by more variety but in many cases less labour intense industrial units. Industrial Govan is but a shadow of its former self; unemployment remains high, especially among young men. As the sounds of shipbuilding have quietened, so is the recognition that other things have also been lost and that different ways must be found to rekindle skills, confidence and community. One organisation that is attempting to reconnect Govan across ages, history and places is Gal Gael which uses traditional wooden boat building as a way of helping to bridge the gaps. Gal Gael operates on the Geddes maxim of folk/work/place!

Meanwhile, the underground still rattles its way under the Clyde, and connects with a bus station that serves a wide area of the south west of Glasgow, Renfrew and Paisley. The possibility of Govan regaining a role as a regional centre may still exist.

In 2008 the successor to Glasgow Corporation, Glasgow City Council, approved the designation of the centre of Govan as a Conservation Area. High quality environmental work at Govan Cross in 2011 may be the first fruits of the conservation area; but it also gives a more positive feeling to an area which has changed over the years. *Sunny Govan Radio* and the *South Side News* (which has taken over the *Govan Press* titles) have helped to put Govan back on the map.

In June 2012 Govan was the winner of the Civic Pride (Best Neighbourhood) category of the Scottish Design Awards – an award decided by a public vote. In accepting the award, Liz Gardiner of Govan's Fablevision said:

'Govan has had two eras of greatness – which is two more than most. The first was in medieval times while the second was when Govan was the centre of world shipbuilding. Now we are poised on the cusp of a third era of greatness. This recognition as Scotland's Best Neighbourhood will be a springboard for that.'

The new Govan is at long last emerging from its chrysalis, and Govan Housing Association – along with its neighbours in Elderpark and Linthouse will be key players.

Johnny – about 4 years old pictured in Luath Street in
1971, now mid 40s. We said that short life
improvement was for the time a child grows up.
Where is he now?

Sources and Further Reading

ASSIST, Gilbert, J. & Flint, A. (1992) *The Tenement Handbook* RIAS Edinburgh

Begg, T.(1996) *Housing Policy in Scotland* Edinburgh

Brennan, T (1959) *Reshaping a City House of Grant* Glasgow

Brotchie, T.C.F. (1938 edition) *The History of Govan* Old Govan Club

Checkland, S.C. (1976) *The Upas Tree* Glasgow 1875-1975 University of Glasgow Press

Craig, C (2010) *The Tears that made the Clyde – well being in Glasgow* Argyll Publishing

Daiches, D. (1977) *Glasgow* Andre Deutsch, London

Dalglish, C. & Driscoll, S.T (2009) *Historic Govan – Archaeology and Development* Historic Scotland

EKOS Consulting Ltd (2008) *Evaluation of the Wider Role Funding Programme* Communities Scotland Research Report 97,

Esher, Lord (1971) *Conservation in Glasgow, a Preliminary Report* The Corporation of Glasgow

Geddes, P. (1915) *Cities in Evolution* Williams and Norgate Ltd, London

Gibb, A. (1983) *The Making of the City* Croom Helen, London

Jacobs, J. (1961) *The Death and Life of Great American Cities* New York

Johnson, J. & Rosenburg, L. (2010) *Renewing Old Edinburgh – the Enduring Legacy of Patrick Geddes* Scottish Centre for Conservation Studies, Edinburgh College of Art/Argyll Publishing

Keating, M. (1988) *The City that refused to die* Aberdeen University Press

Grove, J. L. (1969) *Improving the Environment* Welsh School of
Architecture

Govan Old Parish Church Kirk Session Minutes, February 1968

Martin, D. T. (1999) *Conservation and Restoration in Glasgow –
the Forming of the City* Edinburgh University Press

McKee, K. (2010) *The future of community housing in Scotland;
some thoughts and reflections* People, Place & Policy

Murie A. (2008) *Moving Homes: A History of the Housing
Corporation* London, Politico's Methuen

Naismith, R. J. (1989) *The Story of Scotland's Towns* John Donald
Edinburgh

Reid, P. (ed) (1999) *Glasgow – the Forming of the City* Edinburgh
University Press

Robertson, D.S (1992) 'Scottish Home Improvement Policy,
1945-75: Coming to Terms with the Tenement' *Urban Studies*
Vol 29, no 7

Robertson, D. S (1999) *Peoples Palaces* Glasgow and West of
Scotland Forum of Housing Associations

Robertson, D.S (2012) 'Glasgow's Community Based Housing
Associations: More accident than design' Paper given at
European Association for Urban History, Prague

Robinson, P. (2011) 'Tenement Improvement in Glasgow' in
Architectural Heritage XXI, Architectural Heritage Society of
Scotland, Edinburgh

Skeffington, A.M. (1969) *People and Planning – the Report of the
Committee on Public Participation in Planning* HMSO
London

Whitham, D. (2011) 'Community Housing and Regeneration:
Government Policy and House Improvement' in
Architectural Heritage XXI, Architectural Heritage Society of
Scotland, Edinburgh

Worsdall, F. (1979) *The Tenement. A Way of Life – a Social and
Architectural Study of Housing in Glasgow* Chambers,
Edinburgh

Young, R. K. (1984) *Les Associations Communitaire pour l'Habitat* AIVN/INTA

Young, R. K. (2003) *No ordinary Minister* Friends of Govan Old, Glasgow

Young, R. K. (2005) 'Cities in Devolution' the Sir Patrick Geddes Memorial Lecture 2005

Young, R. K. (2010) 'Towards a New Architecture? Towards a new Society?' in *Scotland: Building for the future* Historic Scotland

Young, R. K. (2011) 'ASSIST in Govan – A Case of Accidental Conservation' in *Architectural Heritage XXI*, Architectural Heritage Society of Scotland, Edinburgh

Index